Managing Business Transformation

A Practical Guide

Managing Business Transformation

A Practical Guide

MELANIE FRANKLIN

IT Governance Publishing

IT Governance Publishing
IT Governance Limited
Unit 3, Clive Court
Bartholomew's Walk
Cambridgeshire Business Park
Ely
Cambridgeshire
CB7 4EH
United Kingdom

www.itgovernance.co.uk

First published in the United Kingdom in 2011
by IT Governance Publishing.

ISBN 978-1-84928-305-2

ABOUT THE AUTHOR

Melanie has an extensive track record in the successful realisation of business change programmes within the public and private sector. She is the founder and Chief Executive of Maven Training and balances her company responsibilities with her interest in helping organisations to make changes that deliver their strategic objectives. Melanie is energetic and enthusiastic, passionate about her job and excited by all of the opportunities that it gives her for meeting new people and hearing about new business ideas.

This book is a result of the many requests that Melanie receives for help in developing an organisation-wide approach for successfully integrating products, services and business procedures that are constantly being created. The ideas in this book originate from the variety of solutions that Melanie and her colleagues have devised to help organisations get better at changing themselves.

There is growing recognition that making change happen cannot be left to chance. Organisations rely on a framework of processes for managing all aspects of their work, but often these don't extend to include guidance on how to change the nature of that work. An effective approach for business transformation is now recognised as a competitive advantage and is regarded as best management practice. Many organisations are now developing their ideas in this field. This book supports these efforts, offering a simple but comprehensive explanation of each step in the business change life cycle.

Each idea is based on sound practical advice that has been stress-tested by lots of organisations experiencing the challenges presented by the increasing demand to offer something new and to do things better.

All of Melanie's ideas are underpinned by a previous successful career implementing large-scale change in the highly competitive, demanding and fast-moving environments of financial services and software development. Her roles have included: developing programme and project management frameworks for global organisations; creating development programmes that build change management capability at every level of the organisation; guiding innovators through the process of translating their ideas into successfully delivered projects; and creating global crisis management initiatives covering 42 countries across five continents.

ACKNOWLEDGEMENTS

I would like to thank the many contributors to this book who have shared their stories and experiences of managing change with me and have helped to shape the contents of this book. Their help stretches over many years and I apologise in advance to any of you who I have not specifically mentioned.

I would like to especially mention Karen Bailey, Arnab Bannerjee, Richard Billingham, Tiffany Childs, Andrew Dangerfield, Fraser Ewen, Simon Fremont, John Gilkes, Robert Grabiner, Paul Jackman, David King, Bruce McNaughton, Polly Murphy, Christine Outram, David Owen, Professor Elizabeth Rouse, Christina Thomas, Fiona Thorburn, Susan Tuttle, David Watson, Clifford Weatherall and Mike Whittaker. Thanks are also due to Giuseppe G. Zorzino, CISA, CGEIT, CRISC, LA27001, Security Architect, for his helpful review comments.

A special thanks to my wonderful family without whose support I would never get anything done, and especially for staying quiet and not reminding me that I promised I would never write another book again!

CONTENTS

INTRODUCTION

This book is for people who are looking for a structured approach to managing change. There is no universally recognised definition of change management, but contributors to this book variously describe it as:

- engagement of individuals and the organisation to enable a smooth transition to a desirable and sustainable changed state;
- all the management activities to successfully move from the current state to the desired future state. These activities include: the definition of the objective, the facilitation of the impacts and the embedding of the change;
- understanding and defining the scope of change required. It includes the planning and successful implementation of the change. It involves engagement of stakeholders working together.

These definitions are of transformational change, which, as its name implies, is about making big changes, often involving many parts of the organisation and affecting customers, suppliers and staff.

Whilst this book has been written to meet the needs of transformational change, some of the ideas are still applicable to incremental change – small-scale improvements that can be identified, authorised and implemented within individual teams or functions.

The structure of this book is based on a 'business change life cycle' containing four stages:

- understanding the change
- planning and preparing for change
- implementing the change
- embedding the change.

The benefit of this life cycle is that it provides a starting point for change and an idea of all the factors that need to be considered. The downside is that it implies that managing change is a logical, linear set of activities. People rarely adapt to a new environment without hesitating before moving forward or revisiting previous steps. However, to make this book readable and enable you to turn to the most relevant section easily, I have tried to set out the most common change management activities in a logical progression.

The business change life cycle is not a prescriptive one-size-fits-all process; it should be adapted to your own circumstances. You might want to consider:

- examining the relevance of each activity to your situation without reference to its position in the life cycle;
- selecting only the activities that are appropriate to your situation;
- changing the order of the activities chosen, adding and amending as you need to, and renaming them to fit in with the words and terms used in your organisation.

If you are interested in understanding the change process from beginning to end then read Chapters 1 to 4, which will explain each stage of the business change life cycle.

If you are interested in the links between project and change management, you might find it more useful to read

Chapter 5 first, so that you can set change management into the context of running a project.

If you do not have formal responsibilities for managing change within your organisation, this book is still of value to you. The ability to define, plan and implement change is a core management skill that is actively sought when appointing people to new roles. It is no longer good enough just to know your job: you are expected to have the motivation and the skill to identify and implement improvements in whatever part of the organisation you work in.

CHAPTER 1: UNDERSTANDING THE CHANGE

Outcomes:	• Impact of the change is understood from different perspectives • Vision of the change is developed • Compelling stories that explain the impact of the change are developed for different audiences
Activities:	• Understanding the need for change • Assessing the environment in which the change will be implemented • Creating initial support for the change

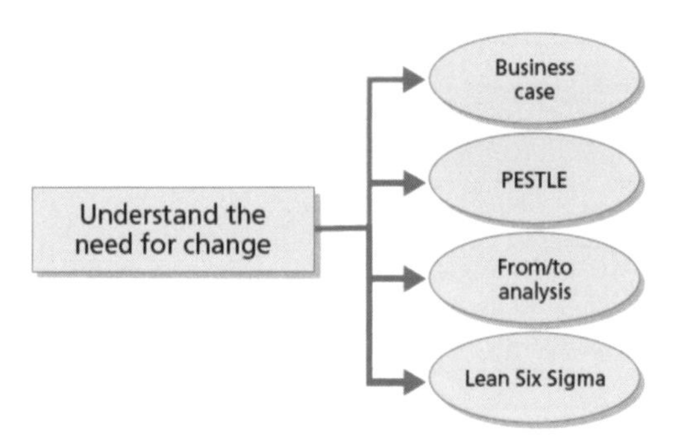

Understanding the need for change

The purpose of this phase is to clarify the reasons for the change and to use this to motivate and persuade all affected that the change is beneficial.

Transformational change comes from the desire of the organisation to achieve its strategic objectives. The scope of the change requires an understanding of the capability needed by the organisation to achieve these objectives, and this scope directly impacts the viability of the change as evidenced by the business case.

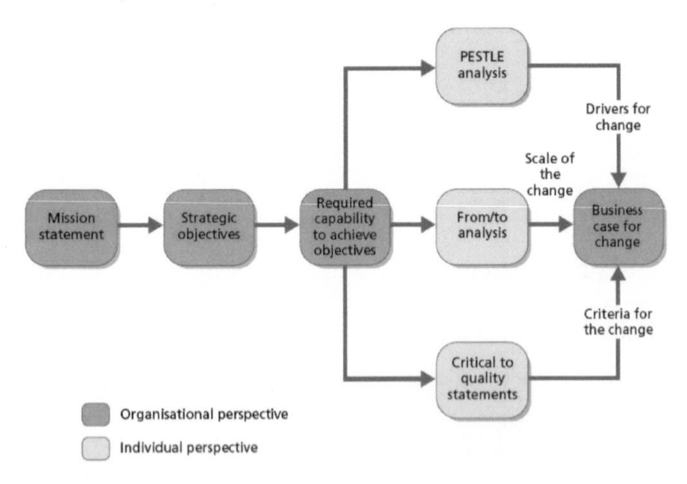

Figure 1: Analysing and understanding change

The process of understanding the need for change is, naturally, at the start of the business change life cycle. However, it is useful to repeat this analysis at key decision points throughout the change to assess its continuing viability.

Those responsible for implementing the change may not have been involved from the start when the strategic objectives are defined, but they are responsible for developing the requirements for new capability, providing a persuasive answer to the question, 'What's in it for me?'

As one of the contributors to this book said when asked what motivated him to implement change:

> Well, I don't go to work every morning just for the chance to make the directors even richer. I change because I want to improve and because I think what I do is valuable to my customers, and I want to give them the best service I can.

This is a typical response – it's personal. People are motivated to change because of how it affects their world rather than for corporate reasons. Reasons for change have to be translated from business benefits to personal statements, identifying improvements, opportunities and solutions to problems.

In assessing change we are trying to identify what the change means – its impact, its benefits and the outcome for the organisation. These reasons will be used to develop support for it by all stakeholders.

A good place to start hunting out the benefits that the change offers is documentation on the reasons why senior management think it is necessary. Look for a **business case**, strategy or position paper that sets out the case for change. Use the benefits as reasons why the change is constructive, and use any information about risks or costs as possible challenges to the change.

Another place to start finding reasons for the change is via a **PESTLE analysis**. This is a mnemonic for identifying the drivers for change:

- changes brought about by **p**olitical factors
- changes brought about by **e**nvironmental factors
- **s**ocietal changes
- **t**echnological changes
- the need for compliance with **l**egislation and regulations
- **e**conomic and competitive forces.

PESTLE analysis is useful in understanding all the possible reasons for making the change, looking behind the internal factors to consider what is happening in the marketplace that the organisation operates in. The information can provide compelling reasons – a 'burning platform' – that is, reasons for jumping to the future offered by the change.

Another type of analysis is called **From/To analysis**. This provides a comparison of the current state (before the change) with the proposed future state (after the change), and gives an indication of the scale of the change. The 'To' statements can be useful in persuading those who are motivated by a move towards a positive future, or who can see that current problems will be fixed.

Translating this high-level information into personalised reasons for change is best achieved 'bottom up'. Present the benefits, drivers and scope of the changes to every level of the organisation and ask the question, 'What does this mean to you?' Individuals provide the details that create credibility amongst their colleagues who recognise the references to, for example, screens and fields in specific IT systems, the activities and tasks from specific processes, or the data on specific reports. Their detailed statements turn bland corporate statements into persuasive, resonant arguments.

Another way of looking at what needs to change is to use **Lean Six Sigma**, which is a set of processes for eliminating redundant activities and increasing customer value. It identifies where information does not flow freely and where there are bottlenecks; it focuses on changes that will improve the whole system, rather than ones that offer improvements in isolation to parts of the organisation.

One of the most well-known aspects of Lean thinking is the emphasis on the voice of the customer. Change is identified by determining customer requirements, rather than starting from the position of 'I have a solution', so let's find a problem that it will solve.

Using Lean principles, the change is articulated as a series of critical-to-quality (CTQ) requirements, which are positive statements of customer requirements.

Case study

An IT company that supplies help desk services has developed a new service to help companies select and install telecoms equipment. The service began 18 months ago and customer demand is strong.

There is a dedicated team of advisers and installers, but follow-up enquiries are routed through the same help desk as all IT enquiries. The service director responsible for the help desk is effectively running two business lines but has seen no increase in staff. She recognises that help desk technicians are increasingly asked to deal with complex telecom enquiries and she has had to invest in additional telecoms training. However, call waiting times continue to increase and customer complaints are on the increase.

Following a review, a company restructure has been agreed that will split the help desk into two units. The service director will retain control of both units and will appoint a manager to run each function.

Business case for the restructure

Benefits:

- Opportunity to exploit potential high-margin business and increase profitability.
- Re-instatement of previously good reputation.
- Reduction of stress, sickness and turnover of help desk staff.
- Increased confidence of the sales team in selling telecoms services.
- Increased customer satisfaction and positive referrals.
- Two promotion opportunities for new managers and clearer career development routes for other staff.

Risks:

- Customers may have to deal with two different departments when they have a complex IT/telecoms query.
- Employees that enjoyed the variety offered by handling IT and telecoms enquiries will be demotivated.
- Investment in training may be wasted if those trained in telecoms work choose to remain in IT, or those highly skilled in IT ask to move to telecoms.

PESTLE analysis for the restructure

Political changes

Continued deregulation in the telecoms industry increases the range of specialist suppliers. Organisations have more choice but they have to procure more than one supplier for the provision of telecoms and data. This is a complicated landscape in which many firms require specialist support and advice.

Environment

Environmental concerns have led to legislation governing the disposal of IT and telecoms equipment. The company's experience in hardware disposal puts it in a powerful position to adapt their service to the disposal/recycling of telecoms systems.

Societal change

The use of mobile technology and social networking requires ever greater access to secure and fast networks. Data available from all telecoms suppliers indicates that this trend will continue to grow in the medium term.

Technological changes

Telephone systems continue to increase in complexity and the need to integrate mobile devices with access to data is growing. Some specialist jobs today did not exist even three years ago. Small and medium-sized firms do not have the capital to hire the wide range of staff needed for telecoms provision and are increasingly turning to outsourcing to access specialist skills.

Legislative compliance

Data protection, system security and access to networks is a complex and evolving area. Establishing telecoms systems that comply with current legislation, and are prepared for future legislation, is a growth area.

Economic and competitive forces

Provision of basic help desk facilities has been commoditised. There are multiple suppliers and strong price competition. It is difficult for any organisation to distinguish itself and charge high prices, and this pressure on margins means that organisations need to look for higher margin business.

From/to analysis for the restructure

From	To
Telecoms queries answered by IT specialists without telecoms skills. Calls take longer than they should, call waiting times are on the increase and customer satisfaction is declining.	Call waiting times are low and customer satisfaction levels in IT and telecoms are above the national average for this type of service.
Staff asked to take on additional specialist work without a formal selection process, and with no additional financial reward.	A clearly defined career path for IT and telecoms specialists. There are clearly defined job descriptions, which identify core competencies for each skill set, and the salaries for each role are benchmarked against equivalent vacancies in other organisations.
Non-specialists sent on intensive, stressful training courses, with limited support in the office, as everyone is still learning and there are no specialists available to provide on-the-job support.	A number of experienced senior managers have been appointed as mentors to support employees before and after technical training courses. There are monthly 'lunch and learn' sessions where technical queries can be shared and solutions discussed.
Levels of enquiry continue to grow as sales teams increase the number of telecoms customers, working hours on the help desk are increasing and so is the average number of sick days per employee.	Additional staff have been appointed for IT and telecoms enquiries, sickness levels have returned to their normally low levels and the organisation is scoring highly in the employee satisfaction survey as a 'great place to work'.

Critical to quality statements

- Customer queries are resolved in a timely manner, i.e. phones are answered within three rings and initial actions are agreed within 1 hour.
- Each query is owned by a single point of contact from the supplier.
- All proposed installations have a project plan and a project team approved by the customer.

Assessing the environment in which change will be implemented

To understand the change fully we need to examine the positives and the negatives and compare their relative strengths.

If the positives outweigh the negatives then there is a ready-made energy and momentum for making the change happen. Effectively those impacted will *pull* themselves towards the new environment. This is often true for changes that reduce customer complaints, or reduce the pressure on individuals to work long hours or in a state of chaos and uncertainty.

Where the negatives are greater, those responsible for implementing the change will have to generate internal energy and motivation to *push* those impacted towards the new environment. An example would be where changes result from regulatory bodies: the change is mandatory, but it does not improve working practices or conditions.

Lewin[1] developed a model of driving and restraining forces to explain this push/pull and warned that we have a natural tendency to restore the status quo, so we need to keep pulling and pushing the change forward until we have broken through our current state to where we want to be. Figure 2 shows what these opposing forces are for our case study.

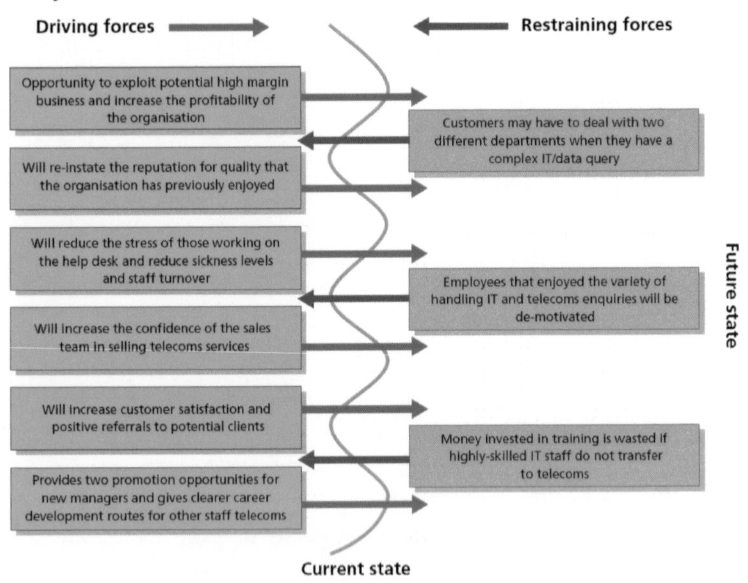

Figure 2: Driving and restraining forces

It is important to understand the environment into which the change will be implemented:

- What is the past history of change in the organisation?
- Is there an expectation that the change will lose energy and focus and never be fully implemented?

[1] Further explored in *Resolving Social Conflicts / Field Theory in Social Science*, Kurt Lewin, American Psychological Association; reprinted edition 1997.

- Do you think employees will feel that they have seen it all before and that this change is no different to the last change that was announced?

The reason for assessing the environment is to understand the challenges that will be faced as you lead people through the change. There are two techniques:

- Maturity assessment – for assessing the environment at an organisational level.
- Change formula – for assessing the environment in the team or department where the change will initially be implemented.

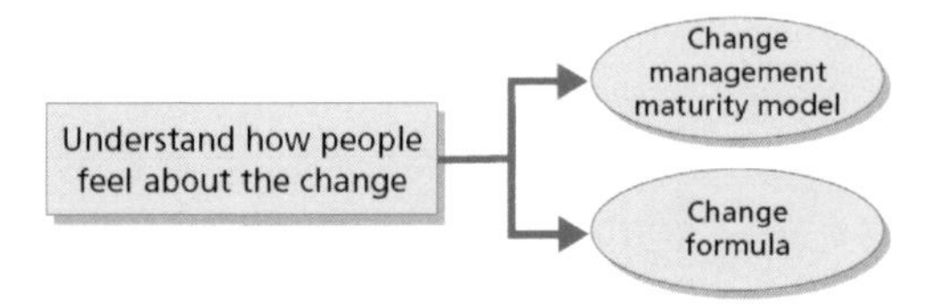

Figure 3: Assess the environment into which the change will be implemented

Maturity model

A maturity model is a structured assessment, usually against five levels of maturity, which enables an organisation to benchmark its current capability (in this case for managing change) and to look at the next level for indicators of how it can improve its maturity.

Evidence of maturity will be sought by asking questions about how change is managed in areas such as:

- skills and competencies

- processes and procedures
- governance
- financial control
- managing the risk
- communicating the need, scope and progress
- resourcing
- measuring effectiveness.

If the results are positive, then existing structures, including those for governing the change management process, resourcing and communication, can be applied.

If the results are weak, then additional steps will be needed to ensure that a framework for governing the change is implemented. This is a significant piece of work, and when planning any type of transformational change, it is essential to understand the scope.

Implementing change in an organisation that sees change as an integral part of its skills and capability is much easier than having to combine the transformation of the organisation with the establishment of a change management framework.

Change formula

The change formula[2] uses a mathematical framework to calculate the likely chance of implementing the change successfully. It assesses support for the change against the perceived effort required. Successful change initiatives will have more support than the effort required.

---

[2] Further explored in *Organizational Transitions: Understanding Complex Change*, Richard Beckhardt and Reuben T. Harris, Addison-Wesley 1987.

The actual formula is:

$$C = [A \times B \times D] > X$$

where

C = change

A = level of dissatisfaction with the status quo

B = desirability of the proposed change or end state

D = practicality of the change (minimal risk and disruption)

X = cost of changing (effort, discomfort, exposure, difficulty, risk).

To apply the formula requires a survey or assessment of those impacted, by developing a series of questions about the current situation (A), the benefits offered by the change (B) and the steps needed to implement the change (D). The answers need to be given a value, and the participants also need to provide their estimate of the cost of changing.

As with many surveys, the answers are the easy part; the difficulties are in creating relevant questions that are self-explanatory and devising a score sheet that enables the interest in the change to be valued in the same way as the cost of the change.

The following example is based on the application of the formula to the implementation of a new patient management system in a medical group of 5 practices, 27 doctors, 38 nurses, and 18 administrators and surgery managers.

To assess the likely support for the change, try using the following questions to understand the strength of feeling about the current situation, whether the change is expected to generate an improvement and whether it is regarded as practical and doable.

To calculate a score for each element use: low = 1, medium = 2 and high = 3.

Add up the scores for every question in the section, and divide by the number of questions to get an average value for that section. This means you can add as many questions to your survey as you like, as it will still result in one value for each element of the formula.

You can calculate the formula for each individual to help you pinpoint individuals who are comfortable with, or concerned about, the change.

You can calculate the formula for all of your colleagues by adding together the scores for each element and dividing by the number of people surveyed. This enables you to include as many individuals in the survey as you like.

Using our change example, the assessment of the change could look like the following table.

Dissatisfaction with how things are now – rate your level of annoyance (A)

	Low	Medium	High
The current system takes a long time to load, especially when looking for a long date range for available appointments			
The current system is not fast enough when finding information for a patient or a doctor, especially when they are on the phone			
The current system does not allow me to specify my queries by name of the doctor or location of the medical centre			
It is difficult to remove data once it has been entered			
We have no reporting from the current system, so cannot track our actions or progress			
Less than 50% of the office know how to use the current system, so all queries have to go to the same people to be answered			

Vision of what is possible – rate your level of excitement (B)

	Low	Medium	High
We can enable doctors to see the patient history for themselves via access to their account instead of having to find the files for them			
We will not have to undertake follow-up calls to patients to remind them of their appointments, as they will receive a confirmation and a reminder e-mail			
Patients will be able to record 'symptom diaries' directly into the system which can be viewed by their doctor			
We can easily track the activity in the system by patients, doctors and administrators via the reporting module			

First concrete steps that can be taken towards vision – rate your level of confidence in the approach (D)

	Low	Medium	High
We can load all of the patient information and check for errors before we allow doctors to log on			
We can enable the staff from one medical centre to log on and pilot the system before rolling it out to all medical centres in the group			
We can test the e-mail confirmations that patients will receive about their appointments before the system goes live			
We can train the sales team and the trainers in the use of the system to test out any bugs before learners log on			

Barriers to implementation – rate your level of concern for each barrier (X)

	Low	Medium	High
Not enough time to practise using the system before it goes live			
Not enough time to discuss in detail the implications of each of the functions and features in the new system			
Changes to my role are not reflected in my job description and objectives			
Changes in information that I need, or information that I provide to others, has not been acknowledged or understood			
I don't know who is supporting the system after go-live			

Create initial support for the change

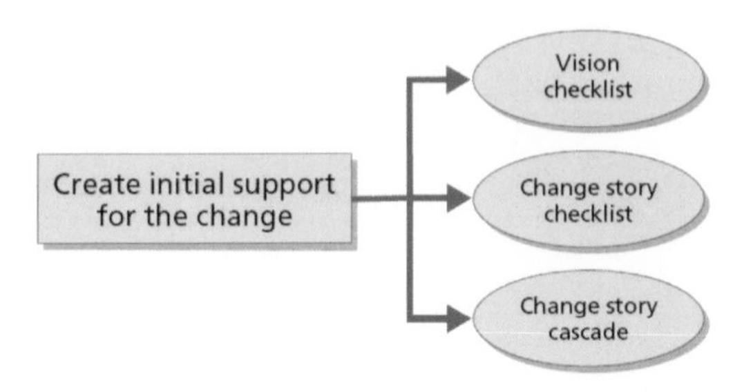

Although 'Understanding the change' is only the first phase in the business change life cycle, it is still important to build a level of support for it. The next phase is to plan the change and this will require significant work and participation from all those affected. If no attempt is made to generate support, it is unlikely that the participation required for planning will be available.

It's also worth mentioning that as soon as a change idea is discussed, even at very senior levels, rumours begin to circulate. The sooner positive messages about the change can be disseminated, the less time that those against the change will have for making their negative views.

The first step in generating this support is to communicate what the change is and what the outcome of the change will be. At a very high level, this can be achieved by creating a vision of the change, which is a short explanation written in very positive language. It's supposed to excite those who hear it, and create a desire to become involved.

What makes a good vision?

Generic criteria

- Written in present tense (we *are* rather than we *will be*).
- Credible and feasible, and its achievement will be visible and obvious.
- Capable of pervading every policy, procedure and action the organisation takes.
- Easily communicated to, and understood by, everyone in the organisation.
- Developed collaboratively, involving key stakeholders.

Future focused criteria

- Clarifies purpose of the change and the direction for the organisation.
- Conveys what the business will look like (in the future).
- Describes what we *want* the organisation to look like in *n* number of years (a preferred and meaningful future state).
- Describes the organisation's future in positive terms (instead of describing what the organisation does not want).
- Describes where the organisation wants to go (but not *how* the organisation will get there).

Organisational criteria

- Builds on the organisation's history and culture.
- Emphasises the uniqueness of the organisation.
- Reflects the organisation's values.
- Inclusive of the organisation's diverse population (reflects more than one or two viewpoints).

- Appeals to the long-term interests of the business, staff, customers and stakeholders.

Inspiring and descriptive criteria

- Gets people's attention and inspires them.
- Captures the desired spirit of the organisation.
- Provides a motivating force, even in hard times.
- Generates excitement, and fosters commitment and dedication.
- Expresses the organisation's aspirations.
- Focuses people on what the organisation looks like when it is meeting or exceeding the employees' and customers' needs.

To create a meaningful vision that is effective across the whole organisation requires more than a short paragraph. There needs to be a cascade process that takes the original vision and adds more detail at each level of the organisation. This involves a two-way exchange of ideas between the person originating the vision and the person or team that they first engage with. Otherwise, there is the risk that as the vision is cascaded through the organisation, the additional detail will lose the essence of what was originally said, leading to variations in the approach to change and employees heading in different directions.

Example of a poor quality vision statement for a university:

- To provide distinctive, high-quality learning in technology, communications and engineering.
- To be strongly engaged with, and involved in, the UK strategy for technology and communications.
- To produce entrepreneurial graduates.

This vision does not persuade the reader that the future will be better than the present. There is no emotional persuasion to change the status quo, as it is merely a statement of priorities. It clearly marks the destination that the university has chosen as its future, but does not provide any excitement or inspiration for travelling there. It does not answer the question, 'What's in it for me?'

A better approach would be to describe the university's vision as:

We have built upon our strong foundations in engineering and developed this into a worldwide capability for technology and communications research and development. We are utilising these strengths to play a pivotal role in creating the UK-wide strategy for technology that benefits our students through the creation of employment opportunities and investment in innovation.

The vision is important as it helps people understand where the organisation is heading. In some cases it can motivate them to take part and to plan for themselves how they can contribute to the change, but it is very high level.

Build a compelling story

To create more detail, there needs to be a story or series of stories that enable people to see what is being asked of them and why it is worth their while to take part.

The story must be persuasive, contain relevant information and convince the team that the current state must end, explaining the consequences if the change does not happen.

The story must be clear that this new direction is the right one – that it is the only sensible option and leads to exciting opportunities.

The story must be simple, positive, using plain language, with no management jargon that is open to ridicule. It must inspire, giving a sense of urgency about the need for change and excitement about the enjoyment to be had from the future it describes.

Sense of urgency – why this change is needed now

- Describe the problems that the change will fix.
- Explain the opportunities that can be exploited as a result of making the change.
- Outline the risks if the change is not successfully implemented.

Desirable outcomes – positive description of the result of the change

- How it feels to work for the organisation.
- What type of work the organisation does.
- How it is viewed by customers and suppliers.
- The reputation it has with regulators and media.

Impact – an acknowledgement of the scale of change

- List the biggest changes.
- Identify those who will be impacted the most.
- Call to action – how employees can participate.
- Brief description of key actions that senior management is taking.
- Options for activities that employees can become involved in.

Linking vision and stories

Leaders at each level of the organisation need to work with their direct reports to translate the vision into a story that addresses the desires, fears and motivations of their team members. Figure 4 illustrates this cascade.

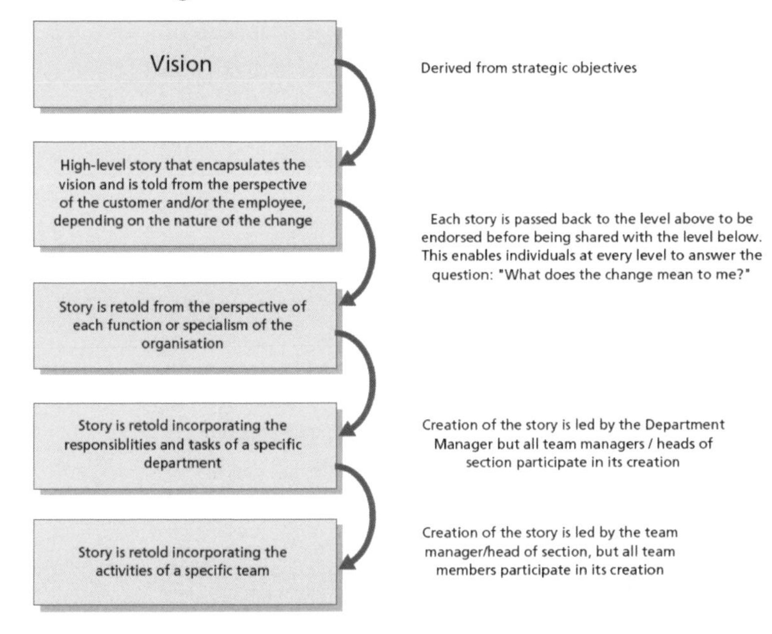

Figure 4: Cascade process

This cascade process produces a number of stories that illustrate the vision told from the perspective of specific teams, as shown in Figure 5.

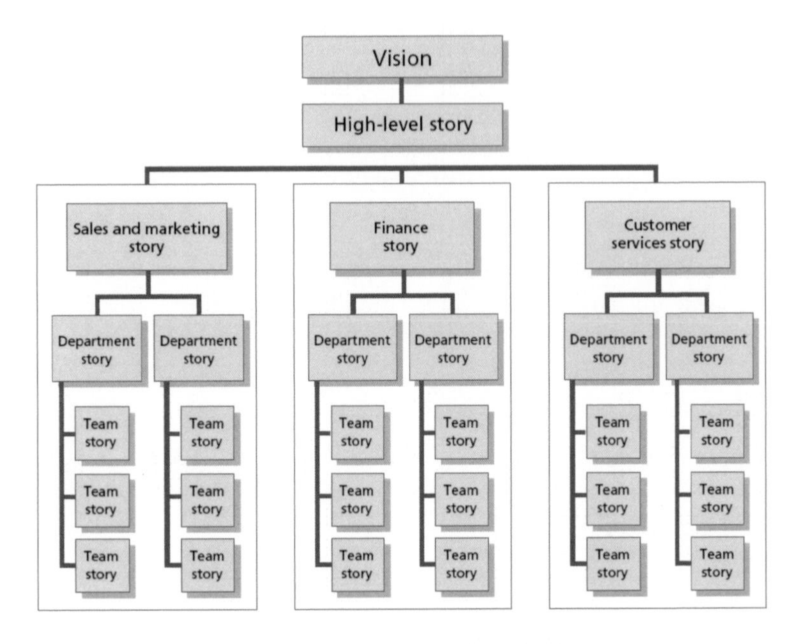

Figure 5: Cascading the stories

The vision and the storytelling combined must:

- Define clear goals for the next 1–2 years.
- Communicate transformation as a compelling story.
- Offer an inspired view of a better long-term future.

The vision and the stories that they lead to are an important part of the communication of change. Delivery of these messages is constrained by the volume of information that a person is able to process at any one time. If you give someone too much information, they become paralysed by 'cognitive overload' – the brain stops taking in further information, and the ability to process, analyse and ultimately understand is impaired.

For effective communication we need to consider:

- What information we provide in each communication – keep communications short on detail, but plan lots of them, each further explaining the change.
- Consider the way in which the information is presented, matching the seriousness of the message with the seniority of the person giving the message.
- Give the listener time to make connections between new information and what they already know.

Case study

A large insurance company made the decision to switch one of its insurance brands to an Internet-only platform. The brand offers a form of home contents insurance that targets those aged 35 years or younger who do not own their own home but own significant amounts of high-value technology.

The change is strategically important as this type of insurance has high growth potential, profit margins are high and there is strong customer loyalty. Compelling reasons for the move include a reduction of the cost base through the elimination of salaries from call centres.

The vision of the change outlined by the chief executive

To meet the needs of our fast growing customer base for TecSafe we will be moving all sales, marketing and customer support for the brand to an Internet-only platform. Customers will be given full access to their own account, enabling them to update their cover, amend payments and print their own insurance certificates and account statements at a time convenient to them.

The story developed by the directors

The move to an Internet-only platform meets the needs of our customer base. Online sales have risen 57% in this year, and 48% in the previous year. Access by individuals to their own account details is the biggest single request for brand improvement from the customer survey, with 72% of customers rating it important or significant. The costs associated with an Internet-only brand are anticipated to be 22% lower than the current cost base for TecSafe.

Customer services and marketing will need to be restructured as they are not currently configured to support an Internet-only brand, and IT changes will be required to provide sufficient online access, security and customer support.

This is a new style of business and there will be many opportunities for staff in marketing and IT to develop new skills to maintain our innovative reputation.

In the marketing department, the story will need to address the winners and the losers – anyone currently involved in online development is likely to be safe in any restructuring, but those responsible for print or event-based marketing are likely to lose their jobs or be asked to retrain in online marketing. This story needs to inspire the 'winners' with the increased opportunities and inspire the 'losers' about other opportunities within the company. Failure to do so risks the loss of those staff who are critical to the success of the brand.

The story created by the marketing director and her direct reports

TecSafe™ is moving to an online only platform, and as a result there will be a significant increase in the proportion of revenue given over to the marketing budget. The current cost base for TecSafe™ is 32% for marketing but this is expected to rise to 65% when we move totally online. Even with a 22% reduction in spend, this is a significant increase in importance for marketing.

Marketing will be expanding its online functions and there will be new roles in Google Analytics, social media brand management, banner design, online copywriting and e-campaign management.

Whilst print and event media are to be reduced, the skills used in copywriting, trend analysis and event origination will still be applicable, and all required training will be provided to ensure that the transition is handled smoothly.

There will be workshops held next week to discuss the new structures. An online survey will be sent to all of you tomorrow asking for your ideas about how you would like to see us expand our marketing services.

The story created by the manager of the events department and his team leaders

There is going to be significant growth in the number of marketing roles available at TecSafe in the next few months. Whilst we are stopping our current exhibitions events from the end of the year, this will be replaced by an online events diary that takes us into new areas.

Our responsibilities are going to move to the creation of webinars, online communities and focus groups of key customers for each business line. This is not an exhaustive list and we will be working in our teams to create an innovative and exciting online events diary.

We will continue to provide trend analysis to the business in customer demand for product and promotional events and competitor analysis, although we will be redrawing the list of target competitors to better reflect online providers.

All of us will have the opportunity to learn new skills and your managers and I will be working closely with Emma in training and development to create individual development plans for each of you.

I am very keen to hear your ideas and would like to invite you to a lunchtime discussion on Friday to air your concerns and ask me as many questions as you want. If you would like to submit questions before Friday, please e-mail me and I will ensure that we post all the answers on the intranet after Friday.

These stories can be used to check the progress and direction of the change throughout the change life cycle. Once a change is under way, it's easy to become focused on the tactical activities set out in the change plan and to lose sight of the end goal. Successful change managers incorporate a regular review of the vision/story into their work. When they have a setback, they can put it in the perspective of the bigger picture, where it will often not feel as significant, and which gives them the motivation to pick themselves up and start again. This regular review of the vision also provides an opportunity to compare up-to-date knowledge about what is happening in the marketplace against the desire for change that may have been conceived in different circumstances and to ask the question: 'Will this change still deliver the benefits we anticipate?'

Techniques for regular review included one participant who had the vision as a poster on his office door that he used to look at every day. One manager held monthly review meetings where he opened proceedings by reading out his assessment of where he thought the change initiative was in relation to the change story, and then chairing an open discussion to hear the views of his team. It gave him a framework for reviewing the bigger picture each month but also forced his team to lift their eyes above the plan and look towards the future they were supposed to be creating.

CHAPTER 2: PLANNING AND PREPARING FOR CHANGE

Outcomes:	• Identification of the activities needed to implement the change, their priorities, interdependencies and clarity over the number and type of resources required • Understanding of who is impacted, how they are impacted and how they are to become involved in implementing the change
Activities:	• Identify the change activities • Establish the milestones • Create the change plan • Communicate the change

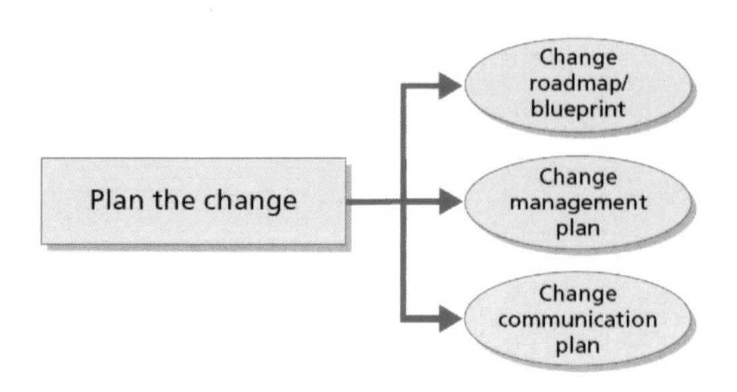

Identify the change activities

Two possible techniques for brainstorming the potential change activities are:

- breakdown structure
- Mind Mapping®.

Breakdown structure

A breakdown structure diagram is used to identify the core achievements of the change. These core achievements are then broken down into more specific achievements, adding more detail as you move through each layer of the diagram, until there is a clear picture of the total change. Once the achievements (milestones) have been defined, the order and priority associated with the milestones can be plotted via a flow diagram.

Mind Mapping

A Mind Map is a diagram that consists of a central core (in this case the change that is being planned) with multiple branches to represent different ideas or thoughts, and in this case, for the possible achievements (milestones). Different branches can be represented with different colours. By presenting ideas in a radial, graphical, non-linear manner, Mind Maps encourage a brainstorming approach to planning in those who like to represent information visually.

Establish the milestones

Change roadmap

One of the problems with making change happen is that many people don't know where to start, which is always a good reason for procrastinating. A roadmap can help to signpost all the steps involved.

The roadmap is not as detailed as a plan; its purpose is to define the major milestones of the change. A milestone can be:

- a statement of a capability that the organisation now has that it did not have before;
- a statement about a task, process or product that no longer takes place or is no longer produced.

Figure 6 demonstrates how these positive and negative milestones can be an irregular pattern, sometimes with more endings of capability than beginnings.

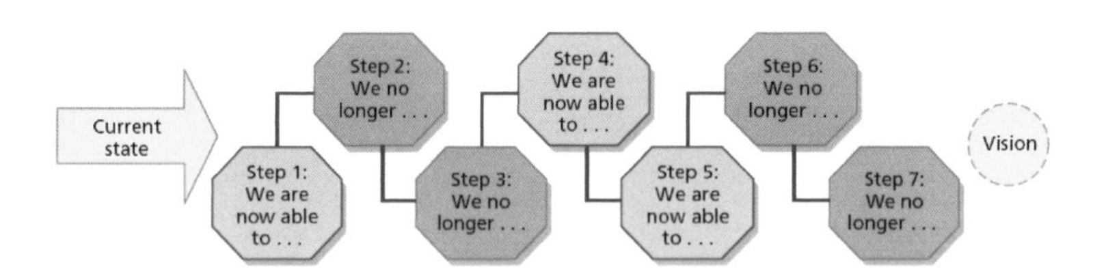

Figure 6: Example of a road map

Use the following statements to generate content for your roadmap.

We have:

- trained staff
- defined processes

- relocated staff
- new suppliers
- new contracts
- new products
- new services.

We are now able to:

- offer existing services to a wider range of customers;
- offer new services to existing customers;
- offer new services to a wider range of customers;
- support a new internal customer;
- process specific types of instruction;
- produce a new type of report;
- increase the information provided by an existing report;
- increase the data that can be accessed by a supplier, customer, internal customer or members of this department.

We no longer:

- attend a specific meeting;
- produce a specific report;
- use a specific system;
- support a specific customer or supplier group;
- support a specific internal customer;
- report to the existing management level or group;
- restrict or remove access to specific data for specific groups (customers, suppliers, internal customers, members of this department).

Blueprint

A popular alternative to creating a roadmap is to create a blueprint. This is a more detailed design of the vision describing the state of the organisation after the achievement of each capability. Different headings are used to describe each part of the organisation, but best management practice from *Managing Successful Programmes*[3] (MSP®) suggests that these headings should be the POTI model, which sets a high level for what must be included and integrated in an effective blueprint:

P **P**rocesses, business models of operations and functions, including changes to operational costs and performance levels

O **O**rganisational structure, staffing levels, roles, skills requirements and changes to organisational culture, style and personnel

T **T**echnology, IT systems and tools, equipment, buildings, machinery, accommodation requirements

I **I**nformation and data requirements, changes from existing to future state, including details of any new developments or redevelopments.

One of the benefits of the blueprint is that its four headings provide a structure for recording the activities in the change plan. However, there are lots of interdependencies between

---

[3] Further explored in *Managing Successful Programmes*, TSO, 2007.

the headings and this can make the blueprint very difficult to write.

If I add a new process, I have to ensure I add in any people, systems or measurements related to them. If I realise I have forgotten one of our systems, I have to rework my processes, organisation structure and data requirements accordingly. This level of interdependence means that ultimately we are less likely to have left anything out, but it does need a high degree of concentration to get it right.

The structure of the blueprint easily lends itself to involving different teams in considering specific aspects of the change, for example, HR and department managers to plot the new organisation structure.

Case study

Human Resources are implementing a new web-based system to manage bookings for training courses and workshops and reduce the amount of paper-based administration. The system offers learners and trainers access to course details and materials online so that learning can take place on demand, and it provides an online community for the exchange of ideas. Trainers will be able to see delegate lists and record results from examinations and tests directly into the system.

The current spreadsheet based system (Asign) will be decommissioned at the end of the change, and the new system (Devolve) will run in parallel for three months as bookings for courses are transferred by the training team within HR.

Breakdown structure

In Figure 7, we have broken down the achievements of the new learning management system into two areas: event administration and course delivery. For each of these areas, more specific milestones have been defined.

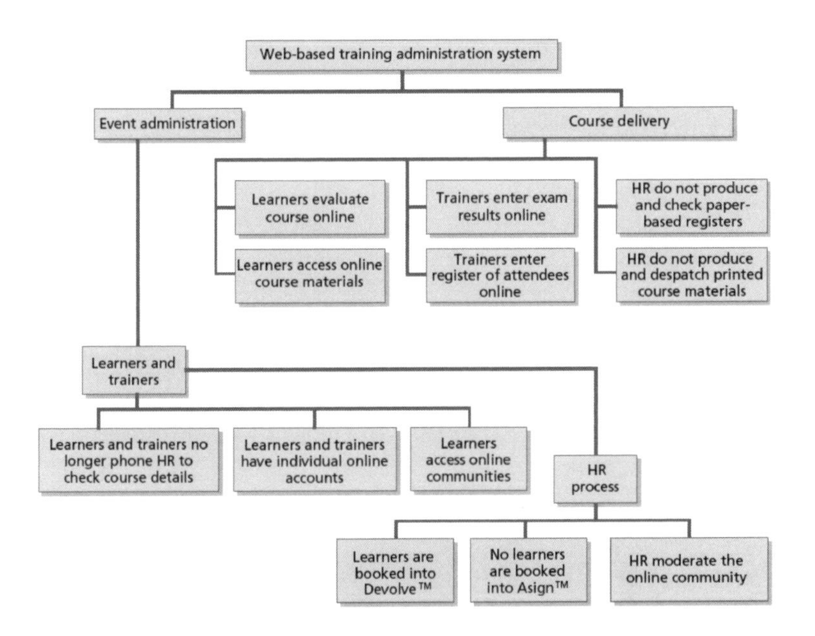

Figure 7: Breakdown structure

Mind Map

In this example, the Mind Map has three branches that show how the learners, trainers and HR staff will experience the new capability.

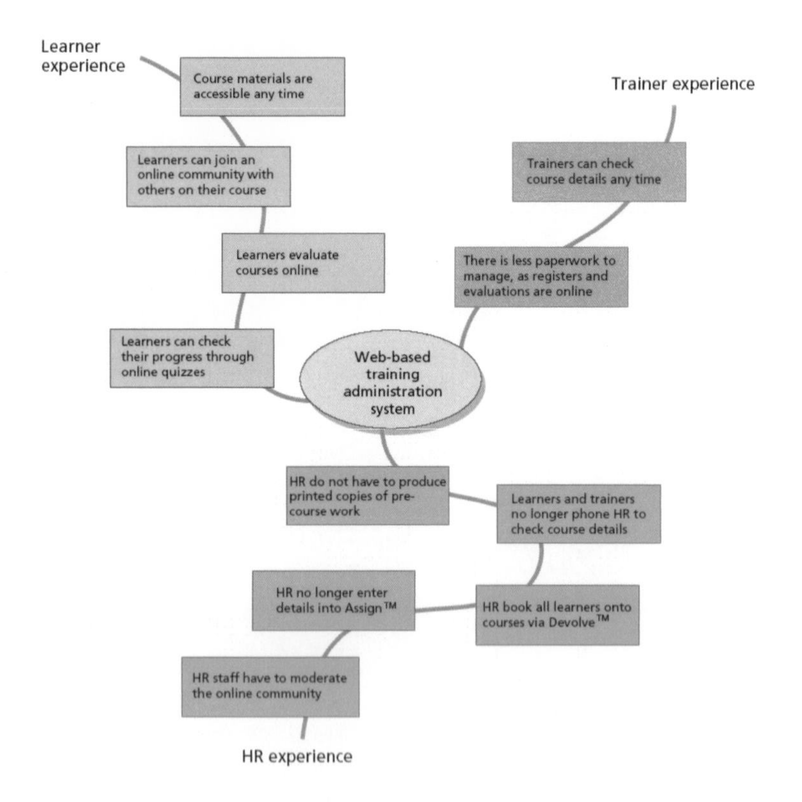

Figure 8: Mind Map

Roadmap

The roadmap shows those milestones that generate new functionality (in blue), alongside those milestones that lead to the cessation of specific tasks or systems (in orange).

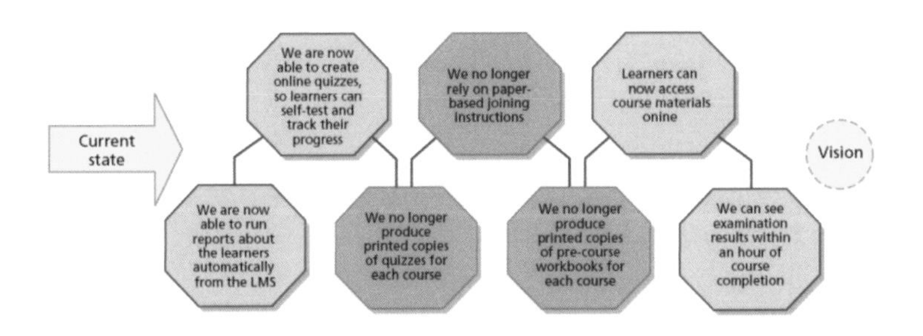

Figure 9: Road map

Blueprint

- **Processes:** Procedures for system security and data protection include items for controlling access to exam results, pre-course materials and online communities.
- **Organisational structure:** Job description for an HR administrator includes responsibilities for online community moderation.
- **Technology:** Devolve is included in the IT architecture plan for the organisation.
- **Information:** Trainers are evaluated on the timeliness of completion of online course administration, including inputting of exam results. Performance of the learning management system is evaluated via measures including:
    - learner access to online pre-course materials
    - online course evaluation by learners.

Create the change plan

The change plan translates the capabilities defined in the road map or blueprint into a set of activities. It is not a project plan as each plan has a different purpose. The project plan identifies, schedules and resources all of the activities needed to create and deliver a change. The change plan, also known as the 'transition plan', 'mobilisation plan' or 'embedding plan', identifies the activities needed to persuade, motivate and engage those impacted by the change to adopt it and embed the change, so that it becomes the new 'business as usual'.

The majority of the activities in the change plan are:

- redefining how work is carried out so that the new system, equipment, procedure or behaviour can be incorporated;
- training employees into how to use the new system, equipment, procedures or required behaviours;
- communicating what the change is, why it is needed and what its likely impact will be;
- building support for the change and a desire to implement it.

There is no set way to structure a change plan. The example used in this book builds on the commonly held view that change has three phases: pre-transition, transition and post-transition, as shown in Figure 10 and then described in detail.

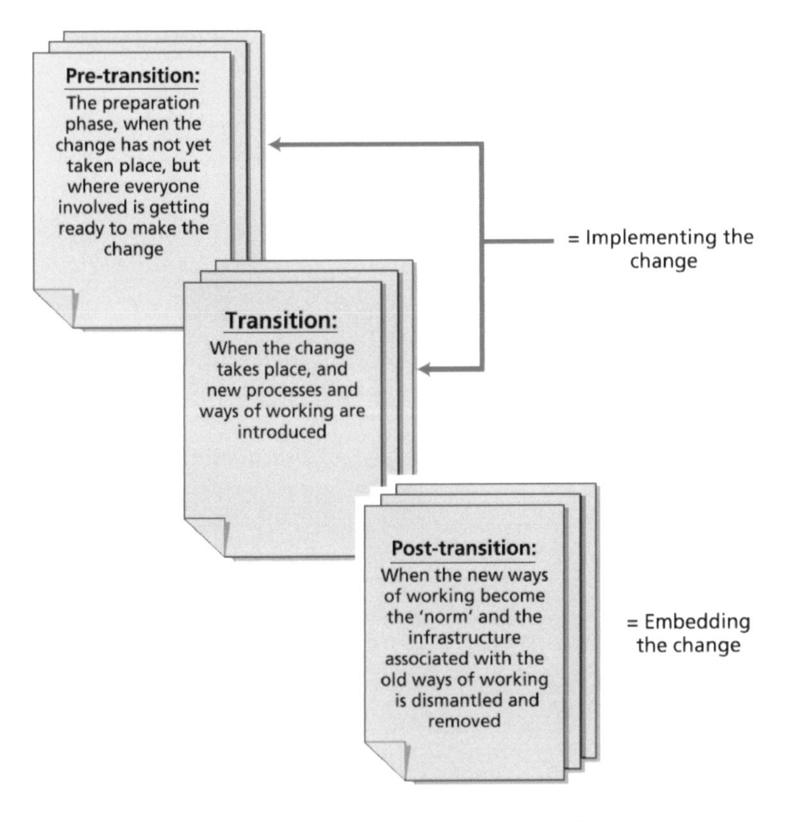

Figure 10: Example of a change plan

Pre-transition

Pre-transition activities attempt to ensure that everyone involved has the necessary information to participate. This includes understanding their role, the activities they are responsible for, who to report progress to and how to report it, what to do if things don't go according to plan, and making sure that they have sufficient time for these tasks.

As one of our contributors explained:

When we know a change is coming, I like to make sure that we have cleared the decks and got rid of anything that we don't need or don't use any more. If there are any tasks that we have been putting off, I make sure we get them done. I don't know how easy we are going to find the change, so I want as much mess cleared up before we start as possible.

Pre-transition is about preparation. Contributors to this book identified three areas that should be addressed:

- preparing the people involved;
- preparing changes to processes;
- preparing performance measures and key performance indicators.

Prepare the people

If there are new reporting lines, new teams to form, new roles and responsibilities to apply then start moving people into these new structures as soon as possible. Even if they have to keep doing their 'old jobs' in the new structure, the sooner that new relationships can form, and new teams establish themselves, the greater the probability that the change will be successful. This preparation also frees people to attend relevant training. Ideally this takes place over a period of time so that individuals can consider how they will apply what they are learning, and raise questions and issues at later training sessions.

Prepare the processes

Effective change is about how things will work in the future, and many contributors to this book made the point that it is the future state that is most important, so it is those processes that need to be mapped out. The following quote illustrates this:

If we begin by mapping our existing procedures, then we are adding no value to what we do now, and we are not making any progress on how we will do things in the future. My staff know their existing jobs, they want to know what will be different so that's what we work on.

It is important to define what is being done, by whom and how the process is governed and by whom and how exceptional items are addressed. Consider the following points:

- What is the trigger for the new process?
- Does this trigger originate from a new source e.g. a new team or a new system?
- What are the inputs to the process?
- What activities transform these inputs into outputs?
- Where do the outputs go?
- Is there any quality control required on the inputs to the process?
- How are the activities assessed to ensure that all steps are undertaken correctly?
- Is there any quality control required on the outputs to the process?
- What happens if an input is incorrect?
- What happens if an output is incorrect?
- What actions are taken if the process is not followed correctly?

Another contributor emphasised the need for 'blue sky thinking'.

We will not make the changes we need to make by amending what we have now. We need to be radical, we need to start with a clean sheet of paper and we need to ask 'what are we trying to achieve' and stop thinking about how we might achieve it.

Although existing processes are near the end of their life, there is still value in identifying manual interventions, duplicate tasks and the creation of outputs that are no longer used. Simply knowing that more streamlined practices are to be introduced can galvanise people into improving what they do now, and this 'bounce' in efficiency can be helpful in creating a positive environment and freeing time to take part in further preparation for the change.

Prepare the key performance indicators (KPIs)

If systems and processes are changing, then current measures of success may no longer be valid. In many organisations measures have built up over time in an ad hoc manner. For example, by measuring how much work is done, or how quickly it is done, enables us to ensure that we are not slipping below minimum standards. Measuring levels of satisfaction, repeat business or order value reassure us that we are meeting customer expectations. As part of preparing for the change, define what levels of service customers can reasonably expect in the new environment, and work with sales, marketing and business development units to communicate these expectations.

There is also a need to specify what internal customers can reasonably expect once the change has taken place, so there are no unpleasant surprises. This also acts as a catalyst for internal customers to amend their own processes to take account of the change.

Performance measures should include the performance we require from others, as well as the performance we expect from ourselves. If there are time, scope or quality criteria that we need suppliers to meet, then these should be established. In some cases, these may be formalised into service level agreements, written into a formal contract and in some cases attached to penalty clauses.

We are a performance-driven culture, so the most important thing for me to get right is how I measure the success of my team. Whatever we are changing, I want to know what the measures of productivity, costs and customer satisfaction are going to be.

Transition

Transition activities make the change a reality. However the change is phased, those doing things differently will require support. In this part of the plan, identify as many innovative ways of providing this support as possible and identify the resources required.

The three types of activity to be included in the transition phase of the change plan are:

- doing things the new way and stopping doing things the old way;
- monitoring activities to ensure that the new ways of working are delivering what was required;
- controlling activities to make amendments to the new ways of working.

Transition can be a time of great stress, as individuals spend time and energy learning new ways of working, whilst trying to maintain their normal levels of work. This normally results in a performance dip, as shown in Figure 11. The gradient and breadth of the dip will be dependent on the level of support received – this impacts on the speed with which they adapt to the new environment. This support can take many forms, including the provision of temporary staff to maintain existing rates of work, or an agreement by management to accept lower productivity during the period of change.

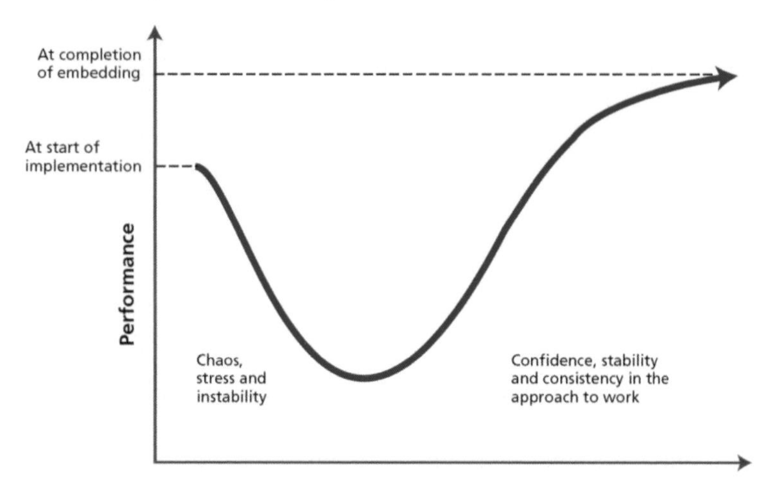

Figure 11: Performance dip

Post-transition

Post-transition activities involve continued support and embedding. In reality, embedding involves removing all traces of the old ways of working, so that when problems are encountered with the change, efforts are made to solve it, rather than taking the easy route by returning to the old ways.

The desire to return to the old ways should never be underestimated. Contributors to this book provided many instances of this, even by those that the change practitioners believed had really adopted the change. Two common prompts for going backwards appear to be:

- The new way of working does not take account of a specific one-off type of transaction that was addressed by the old processes.
- There is concern that new processes are not fast enough to cope, for example during financial year end or during the busiest sales periods, creating pressure points.

Sometimes this return to the old systems, reports or processes is the first step in a gradual return to many of the old ways of working.

Planning checklist

In creating a change plan, we are attempting to predict every activity needed to realise the vision of the change. As we cannot predict the future, we need to remember that:

- Our plan will contain activities that are not required.
- Our plan will miss out a lot of activities that turn out to be essential.

Nevertheless, we do need some idea of what to do, when to do it and who should be doing it, but we should consider:

- An effective change plan will draw in ideas from top-down and bottom-up – the plan cannot come from a single source as no one has all the requisite knowledge.
- The plan will evolve throughout the change, so there will be many versions of it, and the first version should not be regarded as set in stone.
- There are many layers of detail, and a workable plan will have a hierarchy of a high-level plan, and more detailed plans beneath covering specific areas of work. Trying to capture everything in one plan creates an

unwieldy document that is too big and too detailed to be used by everyone involved.

- Multiple versions and multiple layers of detail require a simple structure for updating, so that as information changes, all the plans remain up to date and aligned with each other.

Throughout the plan – pre-, during and post-transition – there need to be points at which progress is formally monitored and where necessary corrective action is taken. As change is so difficult to predict, corrective action often includes identifying additional activities and/or agreeing that some activities are no longer required. This fluidity is essential in responding to the reality of the change as it evolves.

Our planner is excellent at keeping everything up to date. As soon as she updates one of the team plans she adds a note to the master plan and if she changes the master plan she assesses each team plan and amends them where needed. She sends a regular email listing each change and which plans have been impacted by it.

A common misunderstanding about plans is that they are a schedule of activities, which specify start and finish times and name the resource responsible for each activity. Whilst this is an important element of the plan, the plan should include more information, as shown in Figure 12.

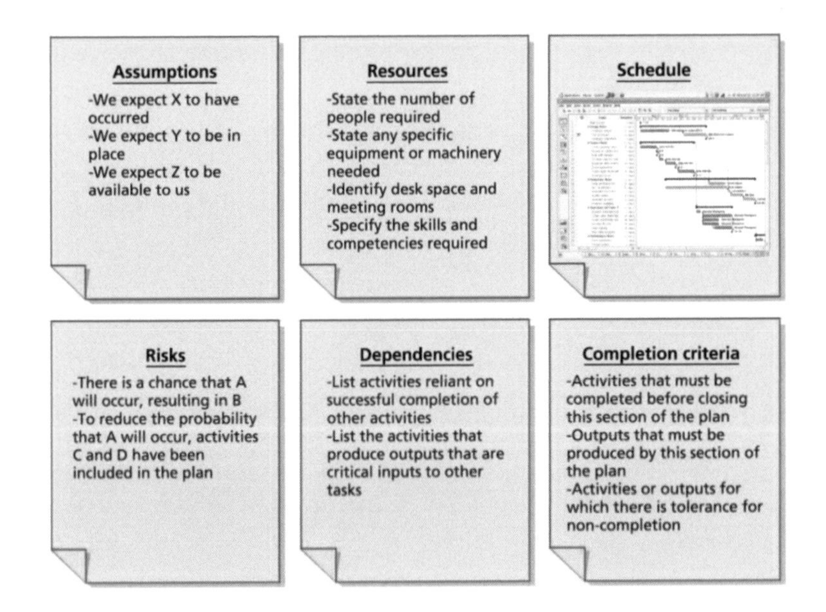

Figure 12: The full scope of a change plan

There is no one right way to create a change plan. In large organisations with significant IT support, you may have access to planning software that automatically tracks progress, sends update emails and enables you to create multiple linked plans, so that when an activity is completed on one plan, all the other plans are automatically updated. In other cases, a simple spreadsheet of the activities involved may be sufficient.

Planning doesn't come naturally to everyone; typically people will produce reasons for a delay in planning such as:

- We need to finish the staff consultation before we can identify the change activities.
- Senior management has not yet agreed the timing of the change, so it is not worth putting a plan together.

However, a plan creates a very clear communication about the change, and gives stability and consistency that people can then adopt into their working lives. They understand what is expected and they know what they have to do, so they can get some control back by deciding when and how to do it.

Communicate the change

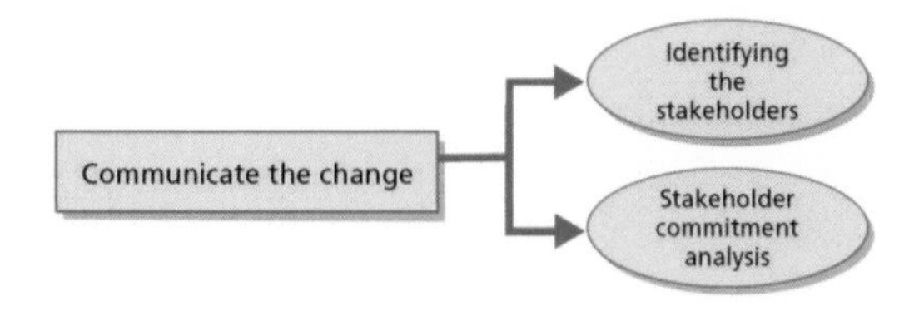

Communicating change is not a one-off exercise – it is integral to every change activity. The techniques provided here can be applied throughout the change life cycle to generate motivation and support for the change and address those concerned with its impact.

Identifying stakeholders

There are lots of different techniques for identifying stakeholders. In *Managing Successful Programmes*, stakeholders are divided into:

- Users – those who will use or benefit from the change.
- Influencers – opinion formers who can influence how others see the change including unions, staff groups and the media.
- Providers – suppliers and other business partners who will be participating in the change.

- Governance – those who manage and control the change including steering committees, management boards, and audit and compliance functions.

Other techniques identify stakeholders by walking through the organisation from its inception, its development of products and services, and delivery to customers. These are supplemented by stakeholders external to the organisation who have an interest in its performance. This start-to-finish technique is shown in Figure 13.

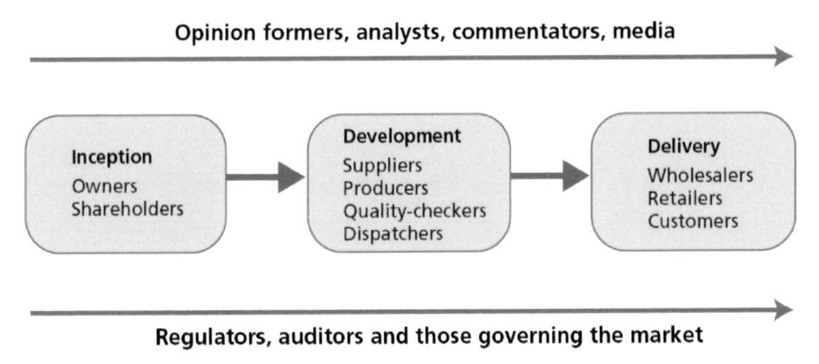

Figure 13: Walking through the organisation to find the stakeholders

Once the stakeholders have been identified, analysis is required to understand:

- What is their level of involvement in the change?
- How much are they impacted by it?
- How much can they influence it?
- What is their level of commitment to the change?
- What is their strength of feeling about the change?
- How much energy and effort are they likely to employ in promoting their point of view about the change?

There was one common thread running through the interviews for this book:

> I don't really care what the stakeholders think about the change – the really important thing is how much effort they are going to put into it. If they hate it, but aren't going to do anything about it, that's OK, but if they hate it and they are going to make time for everyone to know why they hate it, then that's a problem.

The appropriate type of communication is the product of a number of factors including the impact of the change and the level of support that it has.

Stakeholder commitment analysis

Assessing the impact of change to the stakeholders

To assess the impact of the change across all stakeholders, use an impact matrix. On one axis, list the type of impact that the change will have, and on the other axis, list the stakeholders impacted by the change. Use this matrix to plot which stakeholders are affected by which impact. For example, customer-facing staff might include call centre operators (business line 1) and account managers (business line 2), where changes in performance levels impact the call centre operators and new contracts affect the account managers. Figure 14 shows part of an impact matrix with the axes as stakeholders across the top and type of impact down the side.

	Internal stakeholders					
	Customer-facing staff			Support staff		
Type of impact	Business line 1	Business line 2	Business line 3	Function 1	Function 2	Function 3
Processes						
Performance levels	✓					
Business models						
People						
Organisation structure						
Staffing levels						
Contracts		✓				
Employee handbook						
Job descriptions						
Culture and values						

Figure 14: Extract from an impact matrix

In the above impact matrix, we have just used ticks to signify the impacts described above. You may want to grade the level of impact as low, medium or high by using numbers or traffic light colour-coding in the matrix.

The two following tables give examples of the axes that can be used.

Examples of the type of impact to use in the matrix are:

Processes • Procedures • Performance levels • Business models	**Products and services** • Products • Services • Suppliers
People • Organisation structure • Staffing levels • Contracts • Employee handbook • Job descriptions • Culture and values	**Buildings** • Use per building • Occupation levels • Mix of office space for manufacturing/production space • Mix of allocated desk space and hot-desking space • Floor plans
Equipment • Hardware • Computers • Telecommunications • Software: • Off-the-shelf • Custom-made • Peripherals • Office equipment • Specialist equipment	**Information** • Interfaces • Information flow • Raw data • Format • Content • Access and security

Examples of the stakeholders to use in the matrix are:

Internal Stakeholders • Customer-facing staff – sales, business development, customer services • Support staff – finance, marketing, production, development • Board – directors, non-executive directors • Executives – assistant directors, vice presidents • Senior managers – heads of function/department, programme managers	**External Stakeholders** • Customers – high value, all others • Suppliers – essential supplies, all others • Governance structure – regulators, auditors • Opinion formers – media, financial analysts

Level of stakeholder support

Once you know the impact, you can begin to consult stakeholders about their views on the change and also begin the process of influencing and persuading them towards a positive and supportive viewpoint (see Chapter 3).

Ultimately, change cannot be implemented without the support of the stakeholders, so you need to consider how to involve them. Their possible roles are:

- Change agent – fully integrated member of the change team responsible for the successful delivery of change activities.
- Advocate – active supporter of the change involved as a consequence of their specialist knowledge. May have a specific role in quality reviewing the activities of the change team, or providing specialist/technical advice to those planning and implementing the change.
- Guide – responsible for keeping themselves fully informed about the requirements for the change, its progress and any issues or risks, and to step in with advice and guidance when they feel they have something useful and relevant to contribute.
- Opponent – opposed to the change and has shown no interest in helping to implement it. Still requires general communications about the change, which they may critique to demonstrate their opposition. Their challenge offers valuable insight into potential risks associated with the change.

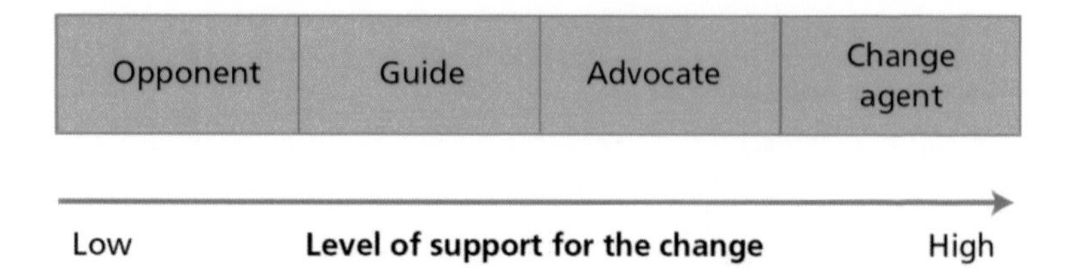

Figure 15: Stakeholder responses to the change

Stakeholder checklist

When assessing the mix of stakeholders, consider asking the following questions:

- Impact
  - Does this change have a direct impact on a process, procedure, system, piece of data or reporting line that you use or are responsible for?
  - Do you have personal knowledge and understanding of the products and services that are to be changed?
  - Do you believe that your involvement with this change will increase the likelihood of successful implementation?
- Agreement
  - Does this change directly contribute to the achievement of your objectives?
  - Will failure to implement this change successfully impact your ability to carry out your role?
  - Are you able to identify any advantages to your role in implementing this change?
- Commitment
  - Do you feel personally motivated to be involved with the successful implementation of this change?

- o Do you see your involvement in the change as additional or integral to your role?
- o Are you willing to present this change to others and persuade them to become involved?

The answers will be influenced by the role of the stakeholder in the organisation. For those in managerial positions, commitment and agreement to the change are more important than how they are impacted personally. For those responsible for making changes to the way in which they work, their interest in doing things differently is key.

Not every stakeholder will begin their engagement with the change at the same time. Sociologists suggest that there are a number of different groups in society who adapt to change at different rates:[4]

- 2.5% are *innovators* – involved in defining the change or taking the lead in implementing the change once it has been identified.
- 13.5% are *early adopters* – not as quick to come on board as the Innovators but still keen to experiment with the changed conditions.
- 34% are *early majority* – find change uncomfortable and will not deliberately seek it out.
- 34% are *late majority* – will wait until a significant 'majority' has made the change before engaging with it.
- 16% are *laggards* – if forced into the change will opt out of it by leaving their job or, if they have the authority, putting a stop to the change.

---

[4] Further explored in *Diffusion of Innovations*, Everett M. Rogers, 1962.

Communications plan

There are usually too many stakeholders to be able to plan communications for each of them individually, so you will need to group your stakeholders. These groups can be based on any factor – for example, location, role, job title or level of support for the change.

Stakeholder Group 1

Date	Awareness			Commitment			Action			Feedback		
	Activity	Content	Outcome	Activity	Content	Outcome	Activity	Content	Outcome	Activity	Content	Outcome
01/11/2011	M	5 mins at end of team meeting to announce authorisation of change programme										
07/11/2011	P	Lunch and learn for the Finance dept.										
09/11/2011	P	Film of the 'lunch and learn' for intranet site										

Stakeholder Group 2

Date	Awareness			Commitment			Action			Feedback		
	Activity	Content	Outcome	Activity	Content	Outcome	Activity	Content	Outcome	Activity	Content	Outcome
08/11/2011				M	Agree who is going to be the lead for each of the change workteams	All teams agreed except HR which will be reviewed next week						
10/11/2011				W	Planning w/s with the change team members							
15/11/2011				W	Planning w/s with the workteam leads							
21/11/2011				P	Lunch and learn with dept. managers							

Key
M = Meeting
P = Presentation (face to face)
W = Workshop
V = Presentation video
N = Newsletter
E = E-mail announcement
B = Blog
SM = Social media including Facebook/Linked in/Yammer

Figure 16: Communication to stakeholders

Figure 16 is an example of a communications plan which plots the detail about the communication for each group against its purpose: leading the stakeholders through awareness of the change; commitment to the change; taking action to make the change a reality; and providing feedback about the change.

Another view of the communications plan is a summary sheet (Figure 17) that shows the type of communication to be received by each group of stakeholders. This can ensure there is a balance of actions and events that will appeal to the widest possible number of stakeholders.

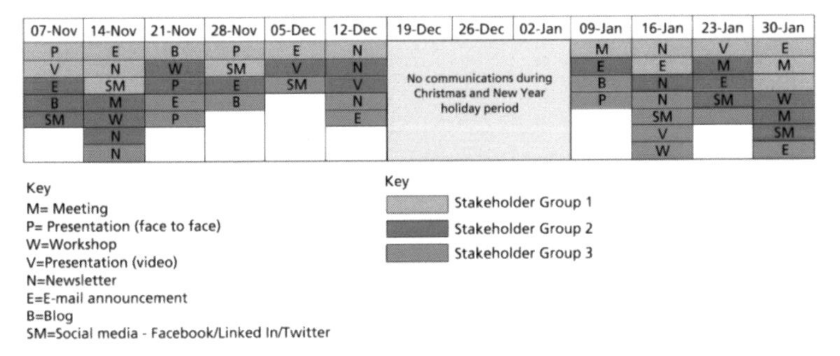

Figure 17: Assessment of balance of communications

The purpose of the communications plan is to convert people to the change. The plan identifies interventions that will:

- persuade people that the change will be beneficial and is something that they should support;
- keep them informed about what is happening, what progress is being made and how the change is evolving as issues, risks and problems become apparent.

Ideally, the activities in the communications plan will evolve from being mostly persuasive to mostly informative. The reason for this is the 'conversion rate' amongst all of those who are impacted by the change.

Wherever possible, use these individuals who are open to change to deliver the communications to their colleagues. Essentially, the activities in the communications plan will transmit enthusiasm, enabling the support for the change to grow.

We got 20–25% of the people affected by the change involved from the beginning. We rely on them to pass on what they have heard to others so that it can spread. This usually gets us invites to other team meetings where we are able to go and talk about the changes.

Communications need to be repeated many times as they are only effective when the person receiving them is in a receptive frame of mind. Many of the contributors to this book emphasised the need for repetition.

I believe in 'redundant' communication – in other words repeating and repeating the key messages over and over. I have learnt over the years that however often I have carefully explained our changes, there are always some who did not hear it the first 15 times and it was only on the 16th repeat of the message that they heard it.

Whilst key information needs to be repeated, the tone and content of each communication will be slightly different as the pressure on stakeholders to become involved in the change increases, as shown in Figure 18.

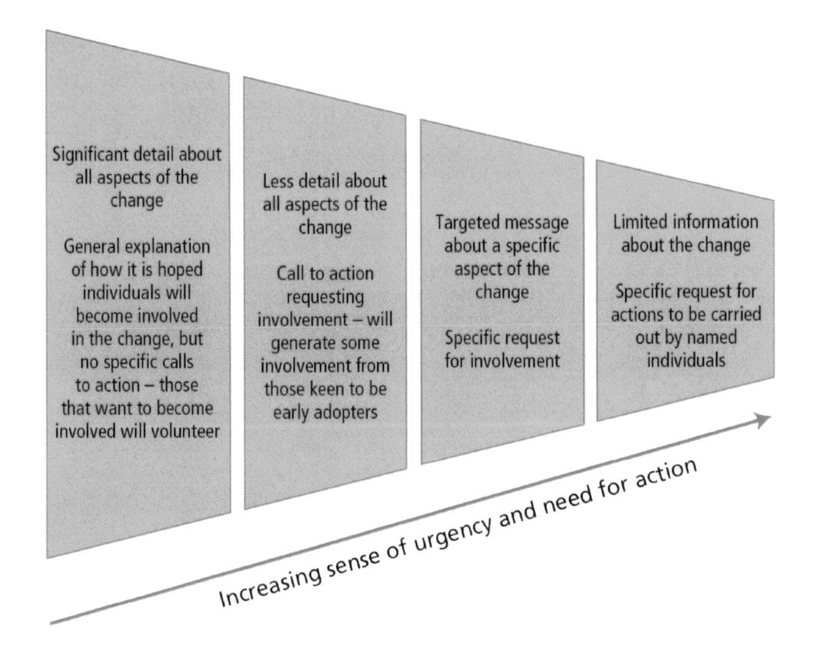

Figure 18: Progression of communication

Continual repetition is necessary to capture the attention of all those impacted by change, and the following Figures 19 and 20 show how communications are transmitted.

When an advocate for the change communicates with a stakeholder, the possible results are:

- The stakeholder ignores the message as they are not yet ready to accept that change is taking place.
- The message is considered and generates a negative response and turns them into an opponent of the change.
- The message is considered and generates a positive response and turns them into an advocate of the change.
- The message is considered but does not generate any positive or negative feelings.

For those stakeholders where a positive response is not generated, the advocate must repeat the communication over time until a response is received.

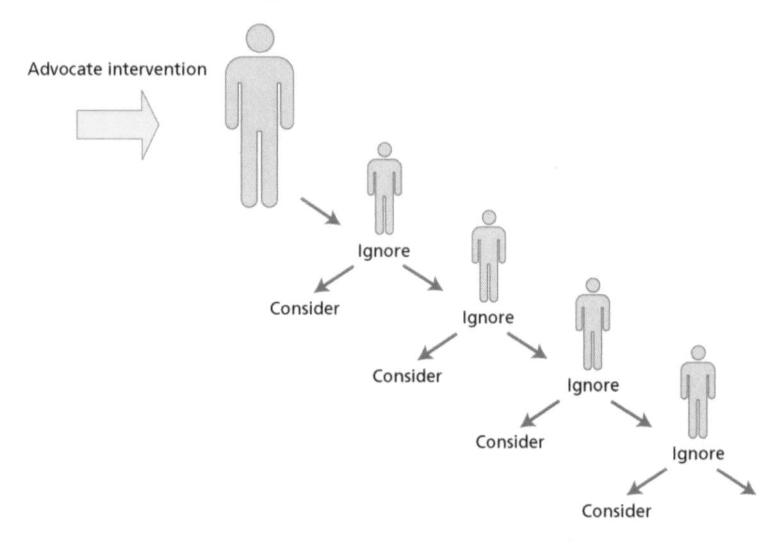

Figure 19: Advocate intervention

If the communication is ignored, further communication is attempted and continues throughout the change life cycle.

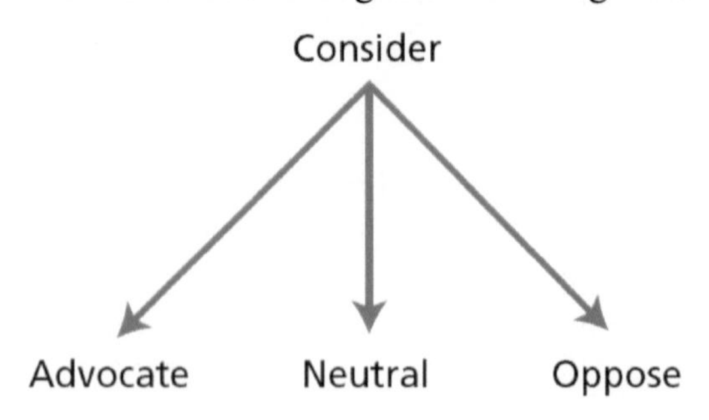

Figure 20: Consideration and response

To maintain momentum during the communication of change, track the success by recording the level of support.

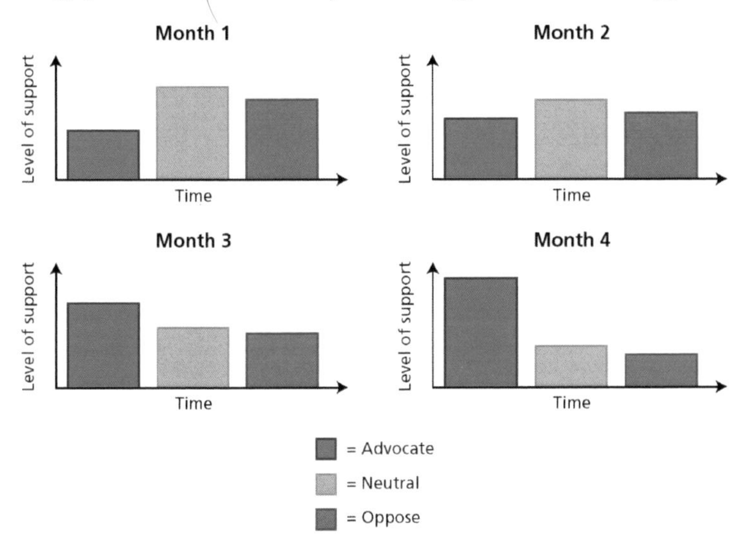

Figure 21: Tracking support

The communication plan can contain innovative ways of communicating including the use of social media. Whatever the medium, the communications need to address the following elements:

- **Benefits** – answers the question, 'What's in it for me?', so talk about the outcomes of the change – the opportunity, what it offers.
- **Reasoning** – decisions are taken by management, but their reasoning can be shared to demonstrate what has been considered: the change is planned and thought through, the constraints that the change is operating within and the forces that are driving the need for the change.

- **Involvement** – provide opportunities for people to participate. There will be higher levels of involvement if people are able to select in which way they participate. Providing opportunities to be responsible for an aspect of the change builds ownership and ensures that individuals are doing the change to themselves, not having it done to them.
- **Expectations** – there needs to be a clear set of KPIs for the future. In the current state, rules (formal and informal) have built up around acceptable behaviour in the office and people need information about the new performance measures so they can identify and create new rules.

There is no substitute for hard work. There needs to be a constant round of consensus building through discussions and meetings. This often means going over old ground and going through the same conversations repeatedly. You have to chip away at it and you have to keep going, even when you think you have said all you have to say. It is frustrating and we will ask ourselves: 'Why do I have to see them again?' and 'Why don't they get it?'

CHAPTER 3: IMPLEMENTING THE CHANGE

Outcomes:	• Change teams are formed to resource the activities • Individuals experience the change and move through a range of emotions as they adapt to the change
Activities:	• Building an effective change team • Understanding how people react to change • Persuading and motivating people to change

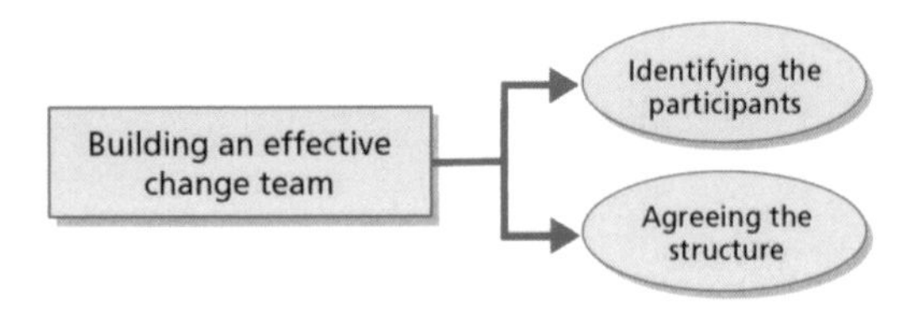

Building an effective change team

The purpose of the change team is to implement the change, ensuring that the change gains maximum acceptance. The change team is formed once the change has been authorised by those senior managers responsible for the strategic direction of the organisation, so it is not responsible for deciding on the scope and validity of the change. This change team is distinct from the project team, who are responsible for the creation of deliverables used as a basis for the change.

Although everyone experiences change differently, there are advantages to bringing individuals together to work through the change as a team:

- Wide range of skills, experience and knowledge – including team members who have experienced change in the organisation before, and those who have experienced similar changes in different organisations.
- Wide range of enthusiasm and energy for the change – those with little appetite for the change benefit from those who are positive about the change.
- Greater level of support for the individuals experiencing the change – not everyone hits the dip in enthusiasm or confidence at the same time, so when some team members are struggling others are there to support them.

In an ideal world, you would be able to pick a dream team; in reality, you have to adopt a more pragmatic approach and use the resources available. Within this constraint, it is important to ensure that there is a mixture of preferences for the way in which work is undertaken, including:

- **Communicator** – this is the person who looks after the team, making sure everyone knows what everyone else is doing. They are the ones we turn to when we are looking for resources or finding out how something works. They are good at picking up on relationship signals; they mediate when there are conflicts between team members and encourage people when they lose their motivation or enthusiasm.

- **Public relations** – this is the person who is good at internal politics. They know how the team should be portraying itself to stakeholders; how the work should be positioned in relation to other initiatives within the organisation.
- **Innovator** – this person enjoys identifying new ways of approaching a problem, and is easily bored by repetition or routine. They are excited by change and actively seek it out, but they have a limited appreciation for how others may feel threatened by change.
- **Worker** – this person enjoys ploughing through the work, meeting the deadlines and ensuring that progress is achieved. They will produce plans and will explain the progress of their work and the team as a whole in the context of these plans. They enjoy routine and structure and will create structure if it does not exist.
- **Fixer** – this person has excellent networking skills and always knows the person to talk to, or who is connected to whom. They can help the innovator to resource their ideas and can support the work of the communicator.

I once worked on a team where we were all alike – enthusiastic, passionate about our work. We played hard and worked hard together and there was lots of after-work socialising. However, we kept missing deadlines and had a reputation for being unreliable. With age comes wisdom and I can now look back and see we were all innovators and ideas people. There wasn't one planner amongst us!

The change manager needs to recognise their natural preference, as this will affect how they manage the team. If an innovator or a communicator is leading the team, for example, they will be looking for support from the worker in terms of plans and scheduling.

As well as the preferences that team members have, they will have differing views about the change. If the change team is to make progress, it needs to have a high proportion of people who are in favour of the change. It is naïve to think that everyone in the change team believes in the value and benefits of the change. They may be involved because of their experience in the job, or their role in the line management hierarchy, rather than as a choice. However, those who are reticent about the change can be useful as they will carefully evaluate its impact, and give plenty of feedback about their concerns. Their views can be used to identify risks and constraints, and give others in the team a chance to overcome this resistance before pushing the change out to a wider audience.

Structure

An effective team needs structure, purpose and an agreed set of processes to enable every member to contribute to the best of their ability. This effectiveness is impacted by the attitude and behaviours of the team members, and, in turn, this is influenced by the culture and values of the organisation, as shown in Figure 22.

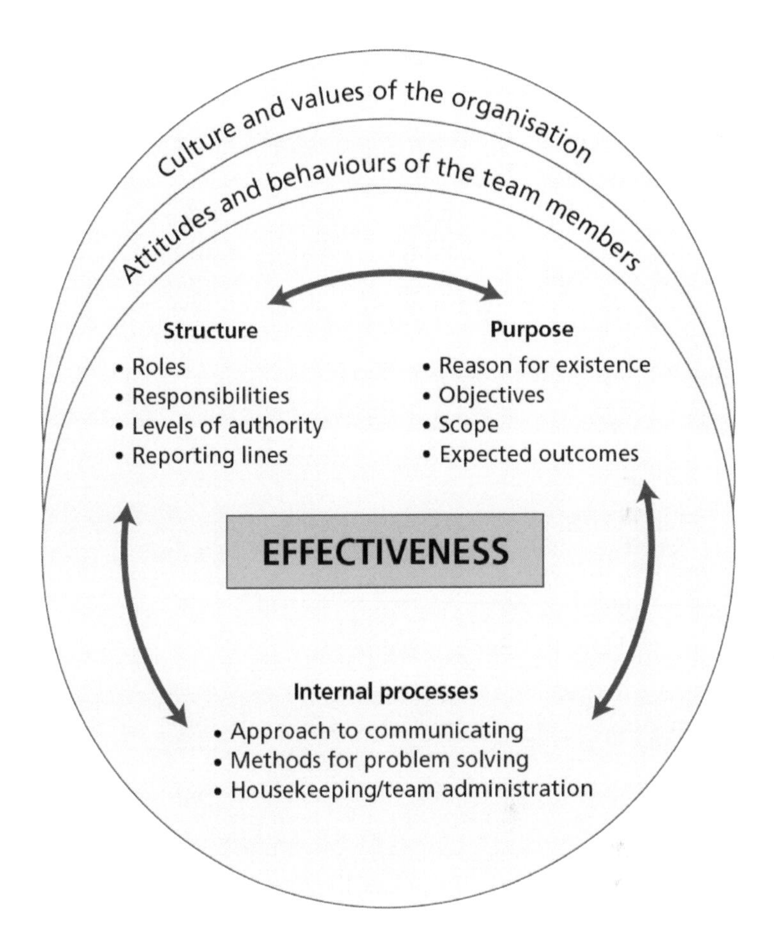

Figure 22: Agreeing the structure

Every organisation appears to have different names and titles for those working in change, so I have summarised the key roles that ensure there is a structure and hierarchy to the change team.

Change sponsor (sometimes known as 'strategic change manager'):

- Senior manager who has the authority to authorise the change, agree the budget for the resources needed and who will report progress of the change to executive management.
- Responsible for creating the vision for the change, and communicating the vision of how the organisation will work once the change has been completed.

Change manager (sometimes known as 'business change manager'):

- Experienced manager who reports to the change sponsor.
- Creates the change plan.
- Identifies the resources impacted by the change – change agents and other stakeholders.
- Assigns activities and responsibilities for developing the change (working with those responsible for project management) and implementing the change (working with those responsible for operational management).

Change agent (sometimes known as 'advocate'):

- Anyone who is responsible for making change happen within their area of responsibility.
- Will be assigned activities from the change plan by the change manager.
- Reports progress, issues and concerns to the change manager and to their line manager.

Resources can be drawn from across the organisation, but it helps if the change manager has a detailed understanding of the organisation, especially those functions most affected by the change. Change agents need to have knowledge of areas that are least understood by the change manager and, ideally, will be drawn from all areas impacted by the change.

We recognise the importance of sponsorship of change but we also need an architect of change – someone who can look at the whole picture and apply the vision across the organisation. This person differs from a change manager in that they have responsibility for bringing the change together across all functions. In some cases, this role is performed by the change sponsor, but in organisations with a mature approach to change management, this role is often permanent, and is at a senior level, reporting to a board member or the CEO.

Scope

The team needs to be clear about the reason for its creation, what it is expected to deliver and the breadth of its responsibilities.

Internal processes

All team members must be clear about how work is done and how information and decisions are communicated. This includes low-level details about the hours of work, dress code, criteria for working from home, access to equipment and technology, etc.

When a team is formed, there will be initial politeness, followed by jostling for position and challenges over the purpose of the team. Once team members start to work together, 'norms' of behaviour will be established and eventually the team should operate as a coherent unit that achieves high levels of performance. The longer the team takes to move through these steps, the longer the wait for it to achieve its objectives.

A team charter is a useful tool in defining the structure, purpose and processes, propelling the team through these early stages and providing facts and specifics for the team members to challenge. Without it, this aggressive, challenging phase will still take place, but the fights will be based on inconsequential aspects of the team, rather than the meaningful 'What are we supposed to be doing?' aspect.

For example, a change team has been formed to implement a change in the invoicing system that the finance team uses. The change is from a manual invoicing process, producing paper copies of invoices and purchase orders mailed to customers and suppliers, to an online web-based payments system.

To develop the team charter, the team asked the following questions:

Processes – how do we operate?

- Should we be located with the finance team?
- What are our hours of operation?
- Are we going to allow home working and, if so, what are the criteria for qualifying for this?

Scope – where does our work stop and that of others begin?

- Are we responsible for the changes within the finance team only, or do we need to include support for customers and suppliers?
- Is it our job to define the reporting requirements from the new software, or has that already been agreed with the software vendor?

Objectives – how will we know when we have been successful?

- Are we expecting all customers and suppliers to transfer to the new system, or will there be some exceptions?
- Are we expected to update the company procedures, or is this still the responsibility of the quality team?
- Will we need to verify the new processes, or is the audit team responsible for this?
- Will we carry out staff training ourselves, or will we brief the training team, so they can roll out a training programme?
- How should we work with IT and the external software vendor?

Checklist for the team charter

- Is the team's purpose aligned with the strategic objectives of the organisation?
- Has the charter been developed with the participation with all team members?
- Has the content of the team charter been reviewed to ensure that all team members have the same understanding of the purpose of the team?
- Have all team members confirmed that they accept the team charter?
- Are the team's goals specific enough to measure performance?
- Do the team's goals reflect the needs/expectations of customers and key stakeholders?
- Do team members understand what tasks have to be done and who is going to do them?

- Do team members know how and by whom decisions will be made?
- Do the skills and experience needed to do the job exist in the team?

In some teams the idea of the team charter is taken further, creating individual 'performance contracts' setting out the contribution of each team member.

Don't overlook the motivation provided by self-empowerment and being responsible for oneself within the team. If you enable people to solve their own problems, they gain confidence about tackling the next challenge. As a change manager, be ready to listen to problems; don't jump in with the answer, but challenge the individual to find a solution. Self-empowerment is vital if the change is to be embedded; but it does require bravery by those leading change teams. The individual will need support at each step, which can up take valuable time.

Understanding how people react to change

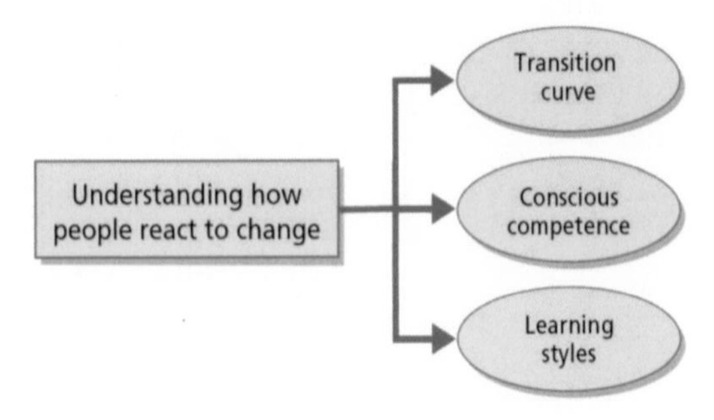

Before we can help people to move through change, we have to understand how they might react to the change. Essentially, human beings react to change in a similar way, whatever the change is. These reactions can be seen as a journey from initial shock to acceptance and adoption of the change, with an associated change in performance as shown in Figure 23.

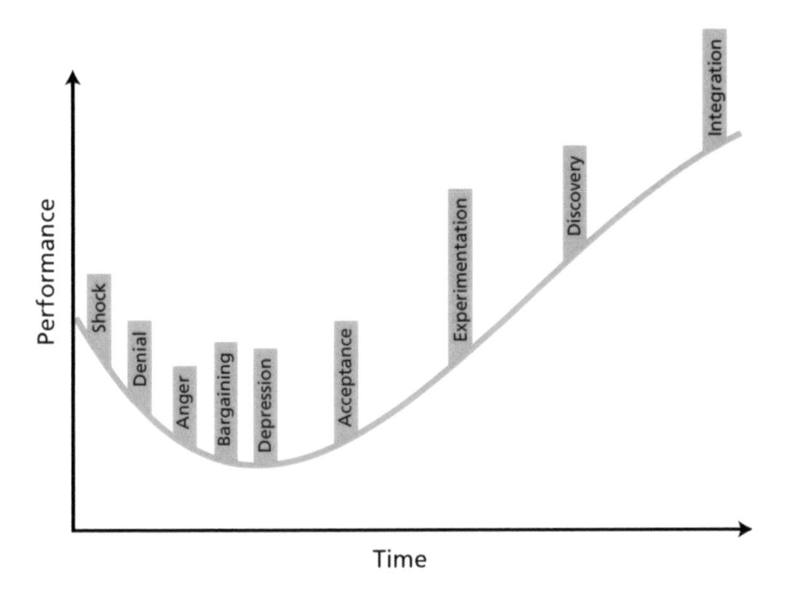

Figure 23: Transition curve (based on the work of Elisabeth Kübler Ross, *On Death and Dying,* Routledge 2008 and Adam, Hayes and Hopson, *Transitions: Understanding and Managing Personal Change*, Wiley Blackwell 1977)

Emotional reactions

The need for new capability can sometimes come as a shock, because up until that point, the way you approached your work was fine. The skills you used and the systems you relied upon were stable, and you had good relationships with your colleagues.

When you hear about a change, your first thought might be that there is a new requirement, but nothing really needs to change because of it. In other words, you are in denial that you need to learn anything new.

When you realise that you are going to have to do things differently and you are going to have develop a new skill set, you might feel angry and annoyed with those that have identified the change. This is because you realise how much extra effort is required at a time when you already feel busy and under pressure.

To limit the disruption to your work, you might decide to bargain with your managers and colleagues. Perhaps you will offer to keep the old system going whilst others make the changes, or you might offer to do other types of work that are not subject to change.

When you realise that bargaining is not lessening the disruption to your work, you might find yourself getting depressed. You might feel more tired at work than usual and want to reduce your workload. You may limit the number of extra tasks that you do, or you might not work past your contracted hours. This has a cumulative effect on your productivity and those around you, and you can sense this in the reduced energy you feel at work.

Cycle of competence

Part of the reason for these negative feelings is the move through what psychologists call the 'four stages of competence'.

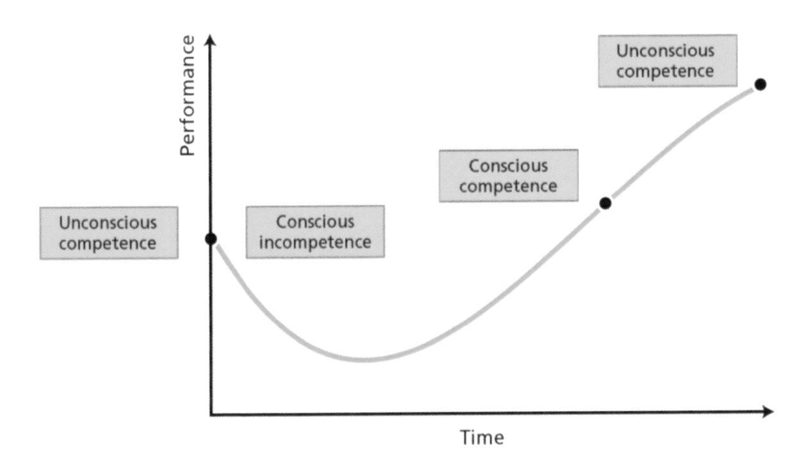

Figure 24: Cycle of competence

At the *unconscious competence* state before the change is announced, you know how to do your job without having to think through every step or consult a checklist before proceeding. This means that you are likely to be fast, efficient and confident in your ability.

The change is announced, and you instantly move into the state of *conscious incompetence*. The knowledge that you have built up about how to do your job is no longer relevant. You are acutely aware of what you don't know – you understand that you are incompetent at the new tasks and the new ways of working.

The move between from here to the state of *conscious competence* will only come as a result of practice and willingness to make mistakes and learn from them. This takes energy and commitment, a burden that was forced upon you when the change was announced.

By practising new skills, competence in the new way of working can be achieved, but it is not automatic at first.

You will think through your tasks and check your work or ask others to do so, as you lack confidence in your ability.

Continued practice will eventually lead to the state of *unconscious competence*. You will be back to full productivity, and because the change was designed to improve aspects of productivity, your competence will make you more productive than before.

When my team are learning a new system, what I notice most is their lack of confidence in dealing with anything out of the ordinary. Even queries that have nothing to do with the new system become a drama, and they will involve colleagues in a discussion of the options. They will often ask me to decide on the action, even though it is well within their level of authority.

Eventually there is a point when you realise that the change is happening anyway, and the best approach is to get involved and stop fighting it. This acceptance enables you to look to the future, and starts you thinking about how you might benefit from your new working environment.

This leads you to experiment with the new or changed procedures, systems, relationships and products, and in doing so, you discover benefits and new ideas that make work easier or more rewarding.

Finally, the change is no longer a change. You have developed new capability, new skills and had new experiences. This new capability has been fully integrated into the way you work.

Moving towards acceptance of the change

Overcoming shock and anger

Communication is needed is to support employees with absorbing the shock and the realisation that what they do now, who they work with, and possibly where they do it, will be different in the future.

They may feel angry that they were not involved earlier in the change, and may feel that the change is being imposed upon them. Some may feel they have been slighted by not being included in the team responsible for exploring the change, because they have special knowledge or experience that would have been vital in reaching the right decision.

Others will concentrate on how the uncertainty between this point and the point at which the change is better understood will affect them. If they are worried about employment opportunities or promotion prospects, this can have far-reaching effects on their ability to plan ahead in their personal lives.

Give lots of background information, so that employees can come up to speed and feel their knowledge is on a par with those who have already been let into the secret:

- Explain the origin of the change including the problem or opportunity that has arisen and why it is important now.
- State who has been involved in identifying the change (the change exploration team) and exploring the options for taking it forward.
- Explain who has been consulted so far, why they were chosen and who else is going to be involved.

- Explain the sources of information that have been used to devise options and take decisions. Explain why this information was selected and what, if any, information was discarded and why.
- Explain the reasons for the decisions that have been taken so far, who took them and any that are still pending and why they cannot be taken at this time (e.g. waiting for the results of analysis or for others to define a strategy or deliver information).
- Explain what is still not known and how this will be addressed.

The shock of organisational change can benefit from the same treatment that we give to physiological shock. We give people somewhere quiet to absorb the information, we give them a hot drink and reassurance that things will be OK, and we give them a chance to talk it through, ask questions and reflect on what has happened. Announcing that someone's working life is about to change can have significant impact, so give consideration to the environment in which you make these early communications, as it will affect how the change is perceived. For example:

- Don't choose a very busy period of work when people will not have a chance to absorb what is said.
- Ensure that either everyone is told at once or make arrangements to meet people one to one, with the request that they don't talk to others until everyone has been notified.
- Provide time and space for people to absorb the information. This includes talking it through or having quiet time to reflect. Whatever the preference of the individual, managers must remember that this is a time

of lower productivity and should manage workloads accordingly.

When our boss's boss called us into a meeting, we knew that the rumours about a restructuring were true. There was a presentation about how our department would merge with the marketing department. I could see straight away that I was being transferred to a new section and that my manager would be Steven, the new events manager who joined the previous month. I cannot remember anything else as I was only thinking about how well I got on with Malcolm (my current boss), that my appraisal was due soon and I was worried that Steven wouldn't review me as positively as Malcolm would.

It is important a safe space is created for people to express their anger without fear of recrimination. Not everyone will be angered by the changes, but it is more effective to allow those who are to vent their anger as early as possible, as this gives them an opportunity to move on.

It's better to flush it out earlier because it will surface somewhere, so you might as well address it up front.

The most effective way of dealing with anger (but the least attractive for the change team) is to hold meetings with those affected. It's no fun being the recipient of this anger, but face to face offers an opportunity to engage with the individual. Establishing online forums can seem like a good idea, creating a community where individuals can have their say; but it can be too easy to whip up a storm and create a disproportionate level of resistance, especially by those who are most angry or most able to articulate their resentment.

Overcoming denial and bargaining

The purpose of this communication is to help employees realise that the change applies to them and that it is something that they will have to engage with. Part of adapting to change is to pretend that it affects everyone but yourself and, therefore, you are not really going to have to change.

I am the head of the department, so I don't need to know how the new time-recording system works – one of my junior managers can input my information for me.

Explain the change so that these reasons can be negated. This means ensuring that the communications specifically address each of the reasons that the individual gives for why the change is not relevant to them. The most effective communication is based on the explanations of the employees themselves and their ability to make the link between the change and how it will help them be effective in the future.

Discuss their position, their role and their skill set in relation to the change:

- Get them to redefine their responsibilities and their job descriptions in light of the change.
- Give them a competence assessment to help them map where they are now and where they need to be.
- Get them to create a training and development path to move them into this new role.

When I lost my assistant in the reshuffle, I was OK about it at first. I was pretty confident I could cope with the work, but I was a bit worried that losing my assistant meant I was no longer seen as a senior manager. It was about a week later that I realised I was stressed. I was short-tempered at work and at home I started to feel nervous about going into work the next day. I booked a meeting with my boss to discuss the situation. I wanted to negotiate a compromise and soften what I thought was a very harsh decision by offering to share Lisa by making her assistant to the team and not just to me. We had a detailed discussion about the reasons for the reshuffle and the need to cut the cost base, and although she didn't agree to the job share idea, I did feel more informed and more involved in the decision to move Lisa on.

Moving through depression into acceptance

Allow people to make the connection between the skills and experience that they have been using and their relevance in the new environment. Reassure them over and over that they will be supported through the change, via training courses, workshops, user groups, and mentoring and coaching. Generate excitement and anticipation about the change by explaining how the new environment will remove the problems and criticisms of the old world.

Supporting integration and experimentation[5]

The purpose of this communication is to get people involved with the change and applying it to their work, so:

- Give people permission to experiment – provide clear boundaries over what they can take decisions about, what they are allowed to remove or add to (e.g. reports, steps in the process, information that is retained or discarded, permission to access information).
- Give them an environment in which they can practise using sand boxes, test systems or pilot programmes. Remove some of the deadlines and constraints of business-as-usual to enable them to do this.

Moving through the transition curve is an individual experience. You cannot predict how people will react, and there is no one-size-fits-all support that will help everyone.

---

[5] Ideas further explored in Adam, Hayes and Hopson, *Transition: Understanding & Managing Personal Change*, Allanheld, Osmun, 1977

To be effective, the support must be tailored to individual needs.

One popular model is the 'learning styles' theory,[6] which explains that we all have different ways of learning about new situations and coming to terms with change. It defines four categories:

- *Theorists* enjoy rational, logical explanations. They review situations from an analytical and objective perspective, rather than using their emotions. We might sum them up by saying that they think with their head and not their heart.
- *Reflectors* like to think things through carefully before they draw any conclusions. They enjoy observing the views and actions of others, but they will not join in until they have decided it's a good idea. They stand on the sidelines initially.
- *Activists* like to get on and do things, rather than analyse the situation. They enjoy new experiences and bring energy and enthusiasm to change, but they can dominate.
- *Pragmatists* are keen to become involved, but their pragmatic approach means that the change has to be relevant to them. Before getting involved they need to see that the change will have some impact on their role.

The motivations of the individual must also be taken into account. There are those that 'work to live' and are motivated by family issues including work–life balance. There are those that 'live to work' and are motivated by career issues and how their current role fits into their

[6] Further explored in David A. Kolb, *Experiential Learning: Experience as the Source of Learning and Development*, Prentice-Hall, 1984.

overall plan for career advancement. Family-motivated employees will evaluate the change in light of their current work arrangements, including the total hours they are away from their family. For their new role, they will evaluate the length and duration of their commute, the amount of travelling they have to do, the location of their office and other important locations, including schools and homes and workplaces of family members.

Career-oriented employees are concerned with career opportunities and will be sensitive to any threats to the trajectory they have planned for themselves and the progress they have decided they should be making. They are interested in any change to their position in the hierarchy. They are typically concerned with:

- the direct reports they will have;
- who their bosses will be;
- their level of authority;
- opportunities to join fast-track management programmes for promotion and for leadership;
- attention and praise from leaders.

The greatest resistance to change occurs when an individual believes that the change is disadvantageous to their current position and/or takes away their positive expectations of the future. Resistance means that they will remain angry, or in denial about the change, or attempt to bargain their way out of having to change.

I was considering the next step in my career when my company announced a merger with one of our largest competitors. I was doing well with regular promotions, had just finished a challenging project and I wasn't sure if I was going to get left behind in the bigger company. I was really impressed to be offered one-to-one career counselling as part of the merger. I had to prepare a portfolio of my work and set out my personal objectives for the next two years, and then I had a two-hour interview with a career counsellor to help me develop a personal career plan, which I then shared with my manager. Two years on I have had a significant promotion and I am very glad I stayed, as there are still lots of opportunities in front of me.

When my company was restructured, we were offered a big spread of options to make the transition easier. I was surprised to see so many 'family friendly' options included in the package and although pay and overtime rates have been frozen for the last year I have been able to change my hours so that I can take my kids to school every morning. This means my wife has been able to return to work part time. It's been a great help, and I don't think I would have been confident to ask if it hadn't been suggested by the company in the first place.

Persuading and motivating people to change

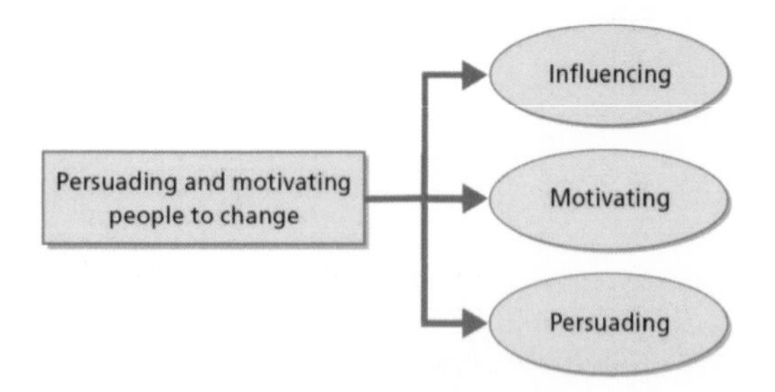

Change is only effective when those involved adopt it for themselves, changing their behaviours, attitudes and patterns of work to create a new environment, one that matches the vision of the change.

To encourage people to make a change, we can use influencing, motivating and persuading. As Figure 25 shows, these techniques have an increasingly narrow breadth of impact.

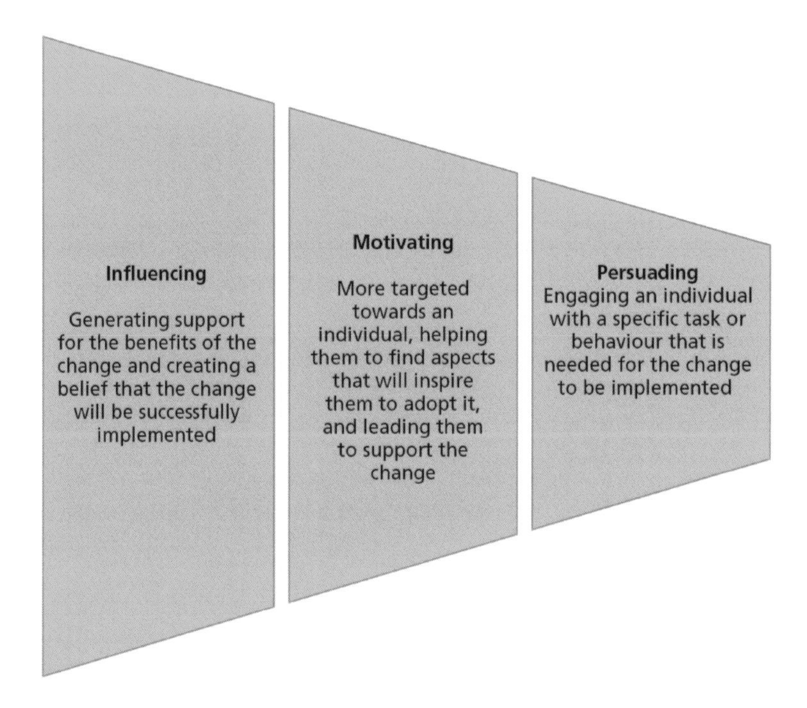

Figure 25: Encouraging change

Influencing

The ability to influence is the power to affect a person or course of events without undertaking any direct action and to be a compelling force on the behaviour of others.

To influence people to become positively engaged with the change requires those leading the change to adopt an attitude of confidence and enthusiasm. The change team needs to create an environment that looks attractive and that makes individuals believe they would be missing out on the fun if they didn't join in. Influencing is, to a large extent, setting an example that you wish others to follow. It is not a direct technique, specifically targeting others, rather it sets out to attract and inspire, so that others are encouraged to follow.

Influencing is strongly associated with leadership skills.

Leadership is the ability to establish vision and direction, to influence and align others towards a common purpose, and to empower and inspire people to achieve project success. It enables the project to proceed in an environment of change and uncertainty.

(*Project Management Body of Knowledge*, Association for Project Management, 2006)

The ability to influence others is directly related to the charisma and personality of those leading the change. Whilst some leaders appear to have star quality, where people are naturally drawn to them, there are techniques for increasing an individual's power to influence:

Be self-aware:

- Understand your own motivation and what attracts you to involvement in the change. Appreciate that this is only one viewpoint and identify other reasons for feeling positive about it.
- Be clear about your strengths and abilities so that you can communicate the complementary skills that you are seeking from others.

Be socially aware:

- Take an active interest in the concerns of others and engage with them, incorporating their solutions into your approach to the change.
- Show appreciation for positive statements and enthusiasm, and incorporate them into your change communications.

- Take time to assess the power relationships before addressing groups and empathise with the emotions expressed by individuals.

The power of influencing can increase through cyclical repetition:

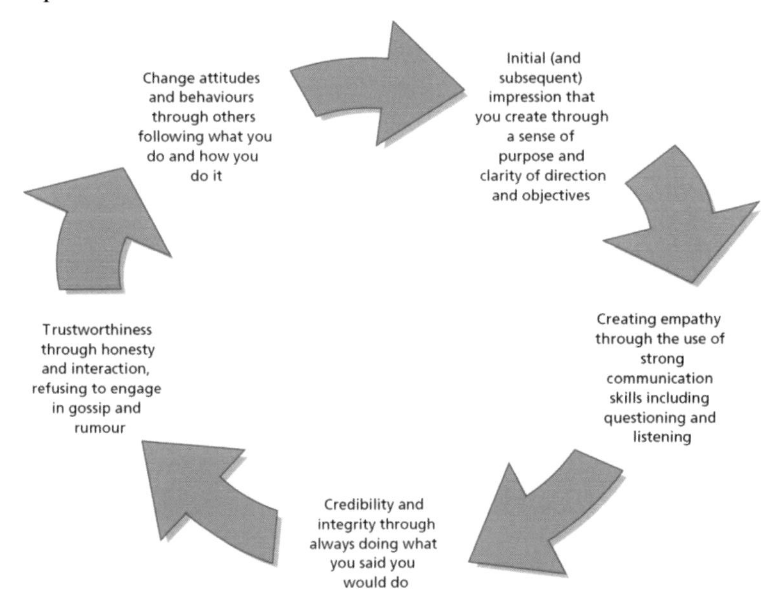

Figure 26: Influencing through the cycle of repetition

Influencing is too hands off to have a direct impact, so it is unrealistic to suggest that you can influence someone from a strongly held negative view to a strongly held positive view. Many models of influencing indicate that its power is to move the views of an individual one position at a time along the spectrum of agreement (see Figure 27). Although the individual you are trying to influence thinks you have the credibility to lead the change, this does not affect their fundamental disagreement with the change.

Stakeholder	Strongly disagree with the change	Disagree with the change	Acceptance of the change	In support of the change	Strongly in support of the change
Stakeholder 1	●	●			
Stakeholder 2		●	●		

Figure 27: Spectrum of agreement

Motivating

Motivation is the general desire or willingness to do something. Motivating others is more specific than influencing. It can generate positive feelings and enough excitement and energy to make the change.

Motivation is linked to control – being motivated to complete a task means that the individual is engaged with that task, keen to plan how to do it and get on with the work. In this way, they are taking control of the task, and are more able to drive themselves through the transition curve.

There are two types of motivation:

- Intrinsic motivation is when we are able to motivate ourselves without an external push – we are doing it to satisfy ourselves.
- Extrinsic motivation is when we do something because of an external force, which might be to avoid a threat (e.g. threat of job loss) or to gain a reward.

Motivation is often a product of both intrinsic and extrinsic forces working together.

Common motivating factors

Common motivating factors are:

- achievement
- recognition
- enjoyment of the work
- responsibility
- career advancement
- personal growth.

If you know in general terms what motivates a person, you can respond to them in particular ways:

- An achievement-oriented person: Discuss the change in terms of what they personally will achieve by becoming involved, and also what the team, department or organisation will achieve as a result of their contribution.
- A recognition-oriented person: Point out who in the organisation and the market place will be tracking the progress of the change (senior managers, potential future employers, respected industry experts) and how individuals involved in the change will naturally come to their attention.
- A person concerned with enjoyment of their work: Highlight how the change will remove existing problems and issues and make the job easier. Enjoyment may be a product of social engagement with colleagues, enjoyment of specific tasks or belief in the value of the work, so discuss the change in terms of these factors.
- A responsibility-oriented person: Highlight how involvement in the change offers opportunities for expanding what or who the individual is responsible for,

and how these opportunities will continue throughout the change as more is understood about the scope of the work.

- Motivating a person interested in career advancement and personal growth: Review the expected skills and experiences that someone involved in the change is likely to acquire. Work with HR and senior managers to identify how those involved in change can apply their knowledge once the change has been embedded. Some individuals will be hesitant about becoming involved in the change because they believe that by joining a change team they are losing their place in the organisation structure. It is the responsibility of the change manager to ensure that the longer-term planning for appointing members of the change team to new roles is agreed at the start of the change.

To ensure that those asked to implement the change are as motivated as possible, we need to aim for agreement with the following statements:

- You feel able to control how you approach change activities – you are able to decide what activities to undertake, and when to complete them.
- You feel that your manager has a good understanding of the work that you are undertaking to implement the change, and that this is aligned to their understanding of what is required.
- You feel supported by your colleagues; there is clarity about what needs to be done and what to do if issues arise.
- You have had positive feedback from your colleagues and your manager on your achievements.

- You feel positive about the change and believe there are benefits for yourself, your team and the organisation as a whole.

Barriers to motivation

If we are to motivate others successfully to become involved in our change, we should ensure that we remove the most common barriers to motivation:

- Not knowing the starting point – lack of obvious structure to successful change.
- Lack of time – individuals struggle to balance their involvement with their business-as-usual responsibilities.
- Distractions – psychologists have counted the number of interruptions picked up by our brain (ringing phones, other people's conversations, traffic noise, etc.) as over 10,000 per day in a busy office.
- Bureaucracy – if the rules and procedures associated with a task are too onerous then creative individuals will feel that they cannot innovate or input their ideas to the work.
- Lack of conviction about the benefit of the change – individuals do not feel that the change means something to them.

When we are motivating individuals to change, we cannot guess what motivates them. The best we can do is ensure that there are positive, motivating aspects clearly signposted in the way in which we present the change.

Persuading

Persuasion is used to get someone to do or agree something that they would not necessarily choose to do.

Persuasion is a process designed to change the attitude or behaviour of a person or group from their current view to the view that the persuader wishes them to hold.

Some people shy away from the subject of persuasion because they are fearful that it is manipulation by another name. However, if people participate in the negotiation of what they will and will not do, they can take responsibility and satisfaction from the negotiation process, which gives them a psychological win.

There are a number of forces at work when we attempt to persuade someone to do something. In change management, our ability to persuade needs to be strong because we are not only persuading someone to undertake an activity, we are asking them to see something in a different light, think about things from a different perspective or adopt a different attitude.

Persuasion is a complex area – we are impacting on the power that someone has over their own choices, so we are reducing personal choice (theirs) and increasing compliance with an external choice (ours). That is why the resistance to change is such a powerful force, because essentially it is about individuals protecting their ability to decide for themselves how their life will be lived.

To understand how to persuade others we need to examine three areas:

- the person making the request;
- the characteristics of the request;

- the types of automatic response that can be generated by a request.

Person making the request

Our willingness to become involved in something is affected by our view of the person requesting our involvement. This view is a product of two factors: liking and authority.

It is fairly obvious that it is easier to persuade someone to do something if they like the person who is requesting their compliance. An essential rule of working in change management is that you need more friends and people that like you than in any other job.

Liking The basics of being liked are:

- physical attractiveness – not much we can do about this one;
- similarity – we like people who are like us;
- lifestyle – background, personality traits, views and opinions;

As a freelance consultant, I work with new teams all the time. I try to fit in, wear the same sort of clothes, work the same hours, use the canteen if my team do, bring my lunch from home if they do – in other words be 'normal' in their eyes so that I don't get branded an 'outsider'.

- compliments and flattery – we tend to believe praise and we tend to like people who provide it;
- familiarity – get them familiar with the change if you want them to like it, and get them familiar with you if you want their co-operation.

When I join a new team, I try and spend time getting to know them and for them to get to know me. I am direct and straight with people. I am clear about how I like to get things done, and I always deliver so they know I am reliable.

- conditioning and association – people assume we have the same personality traits as our friends; you are known by the company you keep.

We cannot always be liked, though. An alternative is to identify friends of the people we are hoping to persuade, and either have them around when we are making our requests or be authorised to mention their name in connection with our request. In these circumstances, we are making use of the power of liking to drive our change forward.

Authority Individuals may participate in change in response to a request from a recognised authority. Authority is conferred as a result of two forces:

- formal authority – job titles, reporting lines, position in the company;
- informal authority – knowledge and experience of the subject.

During change, when everything is new and unknown, there is an opportunity to develop informal authority by becoming an expert in all aspects of the change. Change team members can take advantage of the authority auto-response by becoming experts in the reasons, impact and risks of the change.

You can use titles within the change team to imply authority, via specialist knowledge, over a specific aspect of the change. Successful change teams appoint individuals to head up smaller teams responsible for each aspect of the change, who can be called upon to give their judgement when individuals are resisting the change and need to be assured that what they are being asked to do is relevant and necessary.

First thing I do when assembling my team is to set out who is going to be the lead on each area: systems – processing; systems – reporting; systems – interface; processes – internal; processes – external; planning lead; communications lead. Then everyone knows who to go to, and each member can develop very detailed understanding of their area so we can call on them for their expertise whenever we hit resistance.

Characteristics of the request

Our willingness to become involved is affected by a product of the activity's scarcity and perceived value.

Scarcity If there are limited opportunities for becoming involved in an activity, it appears more attractive. Scarcity introduces a competitive element, a chance that you might lose out to someone else getting in before you.

Whilst it may feel counter-intuitive, to increase participation in change activities, try and create an impression of scarcity. Limit the number of places on a workshop or limit the number of workshops to increase their attractiveness. The value of this response can be diluted if it is overused, so give consideration to the aspects of the change that you think would benefit the most from this extra focus. Good examples include the number of available positions on the change team, where you want to stimulate a competitive element that will ensure that the team members that you select are from the most engaged participants.

Perceived value We all have a natural ability to assign value to our efforts. If we believe that we are well rewarded, then our enthusiasm for taking action is high.

In terms of change activities, we can create opportunities for taking part that make people believe that the effort is well rewarded. For example, ensure that those who are consistently working late as a result of the change activities are given additional time off or the first choice of holiday weeks in the annual rota. Attendance at workshops can be rewarded by certificates of attendance that form part of the individual's staff file and contribute towards their annual performance review.

Perceived value is also a product of comparison. If we are asked to compare two items, the view we take about the second item will be impacted by the assessment we made of the first item.

To use this to best effect, if we are looking for involvement, it's a good idea to present the request that involves the most effort first, so that subsequent requests look less significant.

A lot of what we put in the change plan needs sense checking, as our estimates of how long things will take are just guesswork! We need the involvement of those who are going to be doing the work to get things right but reviewing a plan line by line takes a lot of time, and the best people to review the plan are often the busiest. I usually ask people to review the whole plan and if I get turned down then I ask them to review just one section of it. After all, something is better than nothing, and sometimes I get lucky and one of them will review the whole thing.

Use Figure 28 as a guide for which technique to use in different situations.

	Not compliant	Compliant
Enthused	• Social validation • Liking If the individual is enthused by the change, but has not yet complied with requests to become involved, then lead them towards involvement by demonstrating how others 'just like them' have already made the change, and increase the chances of compliance by getting those that they like to make the requests for their involvement.	• Consistency If the individual is enthusiastically involved in the change, offer further oppotunities for the individual to participate, strengthening their involvement and maintaining consistency with their earlier involvement.
Not enthused	• Authority • Reciprocity If the individual is not enthused about the change, and is not complying with requests from the change team, then 'force' involvement by invoking the authority of others to request the individual's involvement, or use internal 'force' to encourage the individual to reciprocate an earlier favour from the change team.	• Scarcity • Perceived value If the individual is not enthused about the change, increase their willingness to become involved by creating an impression that these opportunities are for a limited period only, or that there are only limited places available. Increase enthusiasm by clarifying the rewards available for those becoming involved.

Figure 28: Matching persuasion techniques to different situations

Automatic responses

There are certain rules that are embedded into us through our formative relationships with parents, teachers and others in authority that most of us have adopted subconsciously, even if we are not aware of them. If we are aware of these rules when we are communicating change, we can apply them to trigger an automatic response from the person we are trying to persuade.

Psychologists recognise three basic rules governing human nature: reciprocity, consistency and peer pressure.

Reciprocity When someone gives us something, it triggers a deep-seated need to give something back in return. In other words, we don't like to feel that we owe someone; we like to equalise the power between us and the other person.

The implementation of change relies on a great deal of extra effort and hard work by those impacted by the change. If the change team uses the rule of reciprocity they can create a group of willing helpers simply by making sure that the helpers are paying back the favours that the change team has done for them.

When creating the change plan and the communications plan, identify actions that will give something to those impacted by the change – create 'favours'.

I was working with a group in the public sector who were short of computers, and a lot of time was wasted waiting for access to the machines on the days when the community workers came in to type up their notes. The change team supplied two new laptops to the community workers and took the pressure off everyone. It created a positive environment and they could not do enough for us in return.

Reciprocity is not driven by equality in size or scale of the favours being offered/received and responded to.

An example is to identify the concerns of those impacted and then create concessions, so the way in which the change is being implemented is adjusted to fit with the needs of the community affected. These concessions do not need to be significant, but they will trigger the reciprocity response; so you have to be ready to request something from the community in response.

Even if your request is at first rejected, when you come back with an alternative request the urge to meet your needs and return the favour is still very strong. Effectively, by coming back a second time, you are showing that you understand that your original request cannot be met, you respect this answer and are no longer pursuing that request. Offering an alternative indicates you have spent time thinking this through and are therefore making an effort. It would be churlish of the respondent not to hear you out and not to review your alternative request.

The second request is often agreed to because in contrast to the first request it appears smaller, which makes the person being asked feel bad about turning down the request for a 'minor' piece of work.

This is a popular technique, and for the more unscrupulous, the initial request is designed to be turned down, almost as a distraction from the main event, which is the second request – the one that is really needed. There is no downside, in that if the first, larger favour is accepted then the change team are getting more help than they bargained for. If the second request is accepted they are getting what they planned for.

Consistency Once we make a commitment we put energy into seeing it through. We convince ourselves we have done the right thing, and put effort into making that a self-fulfilling prophecy.

We are more emotionally attached to something that we have chosen to do than if it were forced upon us. So our role is to ensure that those impacted by change are signing up for the change management activities that we have planned for them. Once we can get them to agree to the activities, the consistency rule should help them to put effort and time into completing them.

You can gain buy-in by asking them to rate how important these activities are to the overall change effort. Next, get the community to identify who would be best to carry out these activities (playing on the desire for personal choice – the community are deciding how the change is implemented). Finally, move in and make sure that those recommended for the activities are allocated to them.

The first intervention is important because it paves the way for future involvement. Again, applying the rule of consistency, if you have been involved in a change action once, what is the argument for not being involved in the next activity? This is called the 'foot-in-the-door' technique.

Another example is to use a 'charter' or 'values statement' as the first step in the change process. By asking people to sign up to a promise about how they will behave during the change, we are achieving that first early step.

Psychologically, a statement is a declaration. By signing a statement we are making a promise about what we will do or how we will behave, which gives us a push to carry out what we have promised. We can use this 'rule' by asking those impacted by the change to define the metrics or KPIs that they think their work should be judged against, and then sign up or promise to aim for them.

Peer pressure One way in which we can persuade people is to tap into their belief that if others are doing it, then they should be too. The logic behind this automatic response is about playing the odds. If we see three out of four people behaving one way and a fourth person behaving a different way, the chances are the three people are correct and the fourth person is wrong.

Another way of putting this is that most people imitate and only a few innovate.

If we want to take advantage of this to implement change successfully, we need to use the power of user groups and reference sites. We are looking for positive examples of the behaviours we want our community to adopt. This is also why we are looking for those most closely connected to the change to model these behaviours.

The evidence we are looking for to trigger the social validation response is not about the benefits of the change, rather that the greater the number of people who have adopted it, the stronger the argument for following suit.

During the tender process I ask software vendors lots of questions about who else is using their system and how similarly they are using it to the way we want to deploy it. I visit as many reference sites as the vendor will give me to hear how the deployment really happened. It doesn't matter how many meetings I have with the vendor – it's the customers that I really listen to.

When communicating change, it helps to have presentations, videos or articles from those that have already made the change. Alternatively, to see it in action, arrange visits by those who are about to change to those who have already changed.

CHAPTER 4: EMBEDDING THE CHANGE

Outcomes:	• The change is no longer regarded as a change – it is now business as usual
Activities:	• Celebrating the new behaviours and attitudes • Supporting those who have not yet accepted the change • Addressing those who will not change

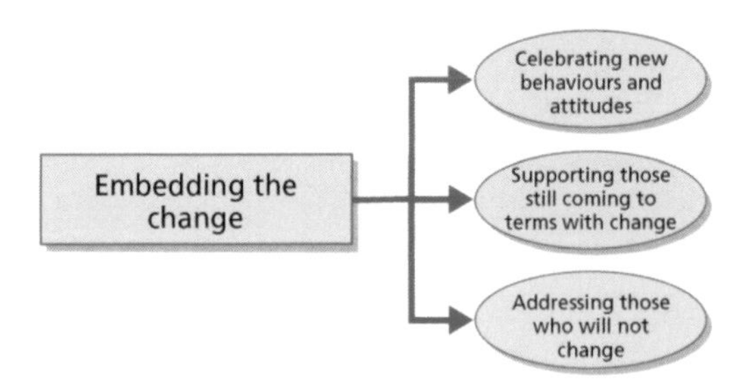

Business as usual

Embedding evolves from implementation of the change and is the point when the change has become 'normal'. It is not yet delivering all of the increases in performance or efficiency envisioned, but there are positive outcomes that can be used to promote continuing effort in making the change become 'business as usual'.

The duration of the embedding phase is hard to predict because it is dependent on the engagement and support of those implementing the change. In successful change initiatives, embedding feels like the tail end of implementing, with just a few tidying-up tasks to complete.

In complex change, embedding is the second wave of implementing, where those already tired of persuading others to change have to re-energise themselves. Momentum has to be maintained through celebratory activities, while the resources needed for support activities must be available to give the change the best possible chance for successful adoption.

In these circumstances, those responsible for the change will be relying on their ability to persevere – to keep going despite difficulties, failure or opposition. Perseverance is part of self-motivation, which is a product of:

- Self-belief – you have the confidence to set yourself challenging goals, and when you hit barriers you are more likely to believe that you can overcome the barrier than see it as a stopping point. To develop self-belief, you regularly remind yourself how you overcame challenges and succeeded in the past.
- Positive thinking – believing that things will come good in the end becomes a self-fulfilling prophecy. You are less likely to leave things to chance, and you are able to inspire followers who gravitate towards your positive energy. You develop your positive attitude by regularly challenging negative thoughts. You will replace statements such as 'This will never work' or 'I am

useless' with statements that include 'I can make this work' and 'I have a track record of success'.

- Focus – you direct your energy to the key tasks; you establish clear goals that you believe are achievable and that you will feel pleased and/or proud to achieve. You maintain your focus by assessing your progress towards your goals regularly and reminding yourself of the benefits of achieving them.

Embedding is an extension of implementing change and occurs when some state of 'normality' has been reached. It is then sensible to remove all traces of the previous way of working. Up to this point, knowledge that existing procedures, systems and information can still be consulted, provides reassurance that they can return to the old world if things don't work out. This encourages people to take the risk of applying the change.

So what are the indicators that change has moved from implementation to embedding? The easy answer is to check that all of the implementation tasks have been completed, have been applied to all activities and have been employed by all staff, whatever their management level. I make this point because senior managers can sometimes be left out of implementation activities, as their role is perceived as being above the change. The same occurs for junior staff who may be excluded because of the perception that they don't need to know about the change yet, as their tasks do not include this system/procedure/technique.

The key questions to ask to ensure that the change is becoming embedded as the new business as usual are:

- Has the use of new procedures and systems been embedded in job descriptions and performance management structures?

Evidence of this comes from line managers and HR managers

- Have all employees been provided with training in the new environment?
  Evidence comes from the training attendance records.
- Is there evidence from each employee that the training has met their needs?
  Evidence can come from the evaluation forms completed after the training.
- Have the number of help desk queries reduced? Evidence comes from help desk call logs.
- Have the number of mistakes decreased to an acceptable level?
  Evidence comes from the amount of rework being done.
- Have employees stopped referring to how they used to do their work?
  Evidence for this is anecdotal.

Embedding involves dismantling all aspects of the old ways of working that have no use in the new environment. This can involve physical removal of equipment, old paper files, deleting old software packages, refitting offices or manufacturing plants. It also involves the removal of reporting lines, alliances, information flows and decision-making structures. Relationships are the hardest to remove.

I adapted to the new IT system easily. After all, I am always downloading apps to my phone! Including the marketing team in our weekly review meeting took me ages to get used to. For the first couple of months, I felt really self-conscious about sharing my ideas for business development, as I thought the 'professionals' would rubbish what I had to say.

Activities to celebrate the new behaviours and attitudes

Initial identification of the options for celebrating success should be included in the change plan so that any financial requirements can be included in the change budget.

Financial rewards

Many of the contributors to this book gave examples of praise and congratulation that were further cemented by financial reward. The monetary amounts were not always high, but money was used in the majority of examples given. Some of the popular ideas included gift vouchers for shopping or leisure experiences, cash awards of several hundred pounds, money for social events for the team involved or charitable donations in the name of the person being thanked.

We had the training team and super-users walking around providing on-the-spot help during the first three days of going live. We gave them all T-shirts with 'Help Point' printed on and they were each given ten packs of Amazon gift vouchers, each worth £50 to give away to anyone who they felt was thinking things through and applying the use of the system to solving issues. Every time they handed out an award they sounded a horn to get everyone's attention and it created a real buzz throughout the entire department. Well worth the money.

Recognition

A number of contributors established an award scheme and gave out prizes in an awards ceremony at some point towards the end of the change life cycle, so that they could provide official recognition of effort and hard work.

When I lead a change, I make sure we have an award scheme that is well publicised from the moment we get started, so that people know hard work and extra effort will be recognised. It's no good keeping it a secret and then springing it on people at the last minute – where is the incentive in that?

Praise

A simple thank you costs nothing, but is often highly regarded by those receiving the thanks. To ensure these thank yous are not empty gestures, ensure they are backed up with evidence of why the change is a success – for example, increases in performance metrics or compliments from customers.

Putting in the new records system was disruptive. It did feel at least for the first couple of weeks that every customer query ended with 'I will have to get back to you as I cannot find your details on our system'. The first time I heard one of our operators handle a call end-to-end using the new system, I could feel my shoulders relax. I went straight up to him to congratulate him – I might have been a bit over enthusiastic, but I was so relieved! I started to believe that perhaps we had not made a huge mistake.

I use my team meetings to highlight examples that we are making progress with the change. I ask all of my direct reports to come to the meeting with at least one example of how things have improved since we re-organised our whole department. It has set up a bit of competition between them, and we feed all the examples into our monthly newsletter.

Celebrating success should be an easy task, but several interviewees wanted to highlight how poorly it is done in many organisations:

We forget to thank our staff for the efforts they are making because we are too busy concentrating on how much further we have to go. But our failure to acknowledge our initial success harms our chances of keeping people sufficiently motivated to continue to make further changes.

Supporting those who have not yet accepted the change

Not everyone will adjust to change at the same pace. This doesn't necessarily mean that they won't ever adapt, they simply need more support to make the jump into the new world.

Some people fail to engage with the change because they do not see its relevance to their role, or how it is better than the way they were doing things before. Some people resist it because it wasn't their idea. Resistance to change may be active or passive. Active resistance can feel easier to address because it is clear that staff are not implementing the change. Clear evidence of where there is push back allows the change manager to engage with the reasons for this behaviour and replan the change activities to increase the involvement and buy-in of those who are resisting it.

Passive resistance is harder to address because its very nature means that it is less easy to spot. It often takes the form of refusal to change. Work is still being undertaken, but using the old ways of working. The refusal is unobtrusive, no fuss is made, but there is a concerted effort to maintain the old order, and not to move to the new way of working. In this situation, any push back by the change manager will be interpreted as aggressive, which can embed the resistance even further.

I once worked with a guy who was still producing three copies of every customer order to file in a manual system for eighteen months after our purchasing system went live.

Overcoming passive resistance can be more time consuming, because it takes time to bring the resistance to light. Multiple types and styles of communication will be required to engage staff sufficiently to draw out their resistance, and the environment in which this takes place is very important. An environment of trust must be created, where staff feel able to discuss how they truly feel if the resistance is to be articulated. For example, staff will look at how those who actively resisted the change were treated. If a punishment regime has been instigated for all failure to comply with the new ways of working, then it is highly unlikely that passive resistance will be explained, but will instead be driven further under the radar of the change manager.

Removing access to old ways of working:

One option to support the embedding of the change is to remove temptation by removing access to old systems or procedures, for example:

- Stop meetings where the purpose of the meeting is no longer valid.
- Prevent access to systems that have been superseded by new software or processes.
- Decommission old systems and cancel software licenses.
- Physically remove old equipment, and archive paper records that are no longer needed.
- Remove old signage and posters from notice boards.
- Remove old process guides, help sheets and change contact numbers.
- Use the new change in all decisions – recognise that the change has now become the new business as usual, by ensuring that it is the foundation of all decisions from this point forward – recognising new resources, new procedures, new technology, etc.

Coaching for performance

Sometimes those with the highest capability in the old way of working struggle the most to adapt. They were very capable because they not only knew their job, but they understood how their role fitted with other tasks and teams across the organisation. When learning any change, we came to understand the immediate task first but it takes longer to re-establish all of the relationships and interdependencies that make up the bigger picture.

Some people struggle to take on the changes through fear of failure. We need to provide reassurance and hard evidence that getting things wrong the first few times is expected and acceptable, otherwise they will never develop the confidence to make the leap.

In these cases, coaching can offer an opportunity to work through the problem, identify possible options and create a plan of how to implement the solution. Follow-up sessions offer a forum for evaluating progress and the creation of further activities to keep up the momentum until the change has been fully adopted.

Coaching is a one-to-one meeting designed to resolve a specific issue relating to performance, behaviour or attitude. When coaching for change, the person providing the coaching needs to be recognised as someone who the coachee can learn from, either because they have already overcome the problem themselves, or because they have a senior level of experience that in the eyes of the coachee confers ability and legitimacy to address the issue.

A coaching session requires preparation. The person being coached needs to be notified about the session so that they can prepare for it. Give as much information as possible to prevent any mistrust developing. Tell them when, where, with whom and why the session is taking place. Define the area of concern to be addressed, and make it clear that the purpose of the session is to examine options for fixing the issue; encourage the coachee to come to the session with their ideas for how to resolve it.

As a coach, prepare for the session in the following ways:

- Define the desired outcome.
- Identify factual evidence about what is currently happening.
- Clarify the gap between what is happening and what should be happening.
- Identify your own ideas for interim steps to move the coachee towards the desired outcome (so that you are better prepared to hear their ideas).
- Identify as many barriers that the coachee might have for moving towards the desired outcome, and try and identify how you would like to see them overcome them (again to help you guide the coachee towards acceptable behaviour).

It's important to remember that this session is a problem-solving session; it is about achieving the outcome and not criticising the person for the current situation. If you do allow criticism to take place, the likely response of the coachee is to:

- defend themselves and their behaviour
- bring out their disagreement with what is being asked of them.

Whilst it might feel good to clear the air, it will not lead to adoption of the change.

During the first session, explain the desired outcome and provide the evidence of where this is not being achieved. Ask the coachee to identify ways in which they can provide the desired outcome. Ask what the barriers are to them doing so and ask them how they intend to overcome these barriers. Draw out the ideas from the coachee and provide encouragement for their approach. Ask them to identify measures of success, making it clear that you want them to be able to identify for themselves that they are on the right path. Ask them to define a timeframe by which they can achieve each step, and if this timeframe is too lengthy, help them to set more stretching targets to achieve the desired outcome in a 'reasonable' timeframe.

Draw up a timeline and a personal action plan and agree a suitable time for a second session to review progress against the plan.

At the second session, review the progress and ask the coachee to identify examples of success. Ask the coachee to identify any further barriers and work through these to develop an updated personal action plan. If desired, arrange a third and final coaching session to review progress and congratulate the coachee on the change that they have made.

A case study

Our sales managers used to get a print-out of the sales data once a month from finance, and they would be expected to produce analysis on best- and worst-selling products. It was an inefficient system because their analysis took up valuable selling time and they were using data up to six weeks old, which made the reports meaningless.

After the implementation of a new customer relationship management system (CRM), sales data has become available real time. The new procedure is for sales managers to review their sales data weekly and identify targets for the next week, which are discussed and agreed at the weekly sales meeting.

Everyone has adapted to the system except Carl, who is still producing lengthy reports of past data using a variety of old spreadsheets. Carl has not reported any weekly targets since the system went live, and Tony, the sales director, has decided to hold a coaching session to get Carl on board with the changes.

Tony: Now that the new CRM is up and running, I expect each of you to report your targets for the following week, so that we can discuss what is selling well and which customers you plan to target. I want us all to know what each other is trying to achieve and open up the options for cross-selling to our customers. Your reports of year-on-year trends do not provide the team with the information I am asking for, and I am aware that they are taking up to a day a week to produce. I cannot have a good salesman selling only 80% of their time. I need you 100% focused on meeting our targets. What do you see as the problems in producing the weekly target figures?

Carl: the new system calculates all the data from the start of the financial year, but my spreadsheets are based on a calendar year so I need to do a lot of data conversion to get like-for-like figures.

Tony: But I am not asking for like-for-like figures, I am looking for predictions of future sales, not analysis of past sales.

Carl: In order for me to predict what I am going to sell, I need to look at what I sold this time last year.

Tony: I can appreciate that this might have been a useful indicator, but as we have re-allocated the customers and developed several new products since then, it is not really a like-for-like comparison.

Carl: No, I suppose not.

Tony: What steps do you need to go through to produce weekly forecast figures?

Carl: Well, I need to create a new spreadsheet and some new calculations.

Tony: What about using the reporting function in the CRM?

Carl: That doesn't give a breakdown by customer type, customer size, product type, product value and longevity of customer relationship.

Tony: But I have only asked for forecasts by product value and type, which is one of the standard reports. This is the only report that the other sales managers are producing.

Carl: But I thought you wanted more detailed analysis?

Tony: No, the value of the report is its use in starting a discussion of how we plan to achieve the targets and how we can work together.

Carl: OK, I can produce that.

Tony: And I need you to stop your other analysis so that you can create more selling time.

(Carl is quiet.)

Tony: Do you agree?

Carl: Yes.

Tony: I can see you are uncomfortable with this. Can you tell me what you think the problem is with not using the spreadsheets?

(Carl gets out some of the spreadsheets and goes through each line of data. Tony listens and explains why each piece of data Carl values no longer fits in with the way in which the sales team is incentivised to perform.)

Tony: So going forward I am just looking for the product value/type report.

Carl: Yes.

Tony: So how will you use the extra time now you don't need to do the spreadsheet analysis?

Carl: I have been thinking about holding some customer roadshows for my medium-sized clients.

Tony: Excellent. Do you have a timetable for this?

(Carl shows Tony the timetable and they agree on some ideas to market the road shows. They agree to review progress straight after the next sales team meeting.)

Creating remedial training events

Rerunning the original training events is unlikely to address the concerns of those who need extra support. Whilst some might appreciate a review of the basics, most will be struggling with specific situations relevant to their role and for which they need detailed guidance. In this case, one-to-one, at-the-desk training is effective.

To ensure the trainer and trainee can get the most out of the session, ensure that the trainee prepares a description of the issues they want to cover and give this to the trainer ahead of time, so that any technical answers can be researched. It is hard to inspire confidence in the change if the trainer does not have the answers!

Addressing those who will not change

There are two schools of thought about those who will not change. One is that they should be ignored, because they are never going to be supportive of the change. They will either leave or adopt the change because everyone else has. The second school of thought is that the efforts to involve them must be high, as winning them over will demonstrate that there is support for change across the organisation as a whole.

Not everyone will want or be able to adapt to the change. Some people are unable to see past their belief that the changes should not have taken place and that the old ways of working were better. Others cannot learn the new approach. There can be no guidance for how long remedial support can be kept in place, but ultimately a decision will be reached that the cost of support and the cost of poor performance (slower work, the cost of error correction) means that the individual must be removed.

Alan always does his own thing and he always gets away with it. If we have a difficult enquiry come in, Alan is no help because he 'hasn't learnt the search function on the system yet' or whatever excuse he is using that day; but he went on the same training as the rest of us – he just can't be bothered to use it.

Many contributors to this book stated that the complexity of EU employment legislation made them wary of addressing the problem, and that in many cases, they spent time and energy trying to find another position within the organisation, rather than start the process of performance managing the removal of the individual. Several contributors noted how many times they had come across failing individuals who had simply been moved to somewhere where they could cause less trouble!

It is a statistical certainty that every change initiative will have some individuals who no longer fit the requirements of the organisation, and we should plan their exit routes as carefully as we plan all of our other change activities.

We should not overlook the impact that those who do not adapt to change have on everyone else. Their failure to comply can lead to strong feelings in their colleagues and their managers.

Those that continue as if the change never happened make me so angry. It's a kick in the face for everyone who worked so hard, and implies that they think our solution isn't good enough.

Successfully embedding change leads to the realisation of the benefits for the organisation and for individuals. Throughout embedding, be alert for opportunities to celebrate success.

CHAPTER 5: ALIGNING PROJECT MANAGEMENT AND CHANGE MANAGEMENT

Outcomes:	• Approach to strengthening the implementation of change through additional project management activities
Activities:	• Understand how change management and project management fit together • Steps of a typical project life cycle to identify relevant change management activities

Understand how change management and project management fit together

Why isn't change part of the project life cycle?

Many project professionals would argue that managing the transition from the current state to a new way of working is within the scope of the project life cycle. Practically, this does not happen, with the activities and effort required to manage the change brought about by the project passed to the users at project closure. This is because:

- It is not cost effective for project teams to remain in place once development and testing of the deliverables has been completed.

- Change activities can benefit from the knowledge of the project team, but individuals cannot outsource implementation and embedding, they have to make the changes for themselves.
- Projects are expected to deliver on time, on budget and to specific quality criteria, but the pace and scope of changes that individuals adopt cannot be constrained in this way.
- The objectives of project and change activities are different. Project activities deliver the potential for change: the new processes, systems, organisation structure, etc.; change activities create the persuasion, motivation and leading by example that results in the new business environment.

Projects and change deliver business transformation

Business transformation requires a combination of change management and project management. Change management defines what is required, triggering a project to create the requirement. The project results in new information, systems and processes which are then implemented into the business environment through change management activities.

Figure 29 shows how change management can trigger projects through the change life cycle, and how each phase of the change life cycle is dependent upon the successful delivery of these projects.

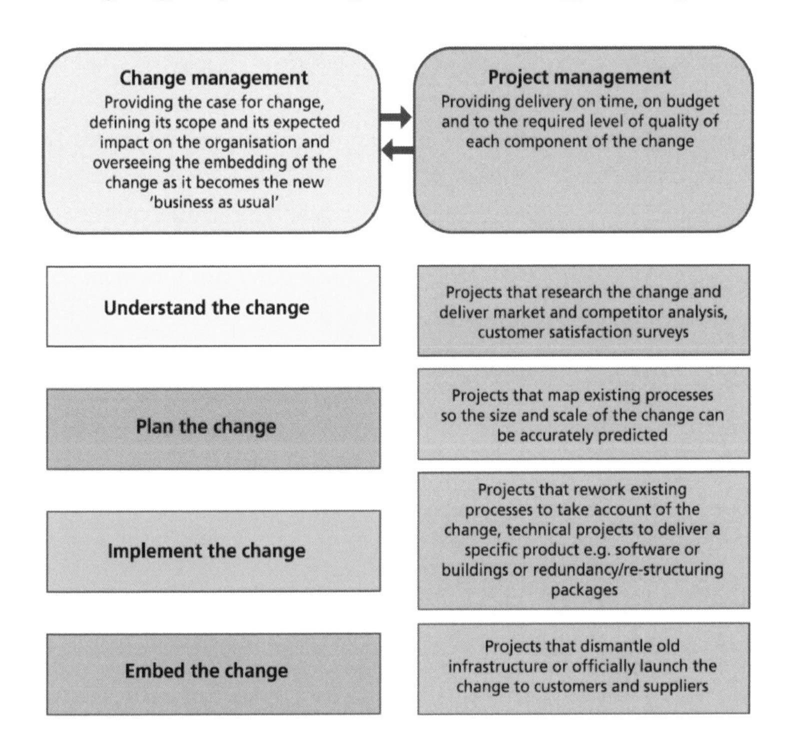

Figure 29: Business transformation

This might make me unpopular, but projects don't come first. They only exist because somewhere in the organisation a decision has been taken to make a change. My organisation has invested heavily in project management training and setting up a project management office, which has given a lot of power to the project managers. But really they are not in control; it's the people who decide that we need to change who are running the show.

Projects do not take place in isolation. They require the involvement of those who will use the project deliverables, incorporating them into new ways of working. This involvement is affected by how users feel about the proposed changes. The vision and stories of how the change will lead to an improved working environment are key to influencing, motivating and persuading individuals to give their time and expertise to the project. In turn, the deliverables and achievements of the projects can be used to inspire and enthuse users to become more involved in changing their environment. Figure 30 shows how the change management techniques explained in this book trigger the need for projects and can also be used to implement what the projects deliver.

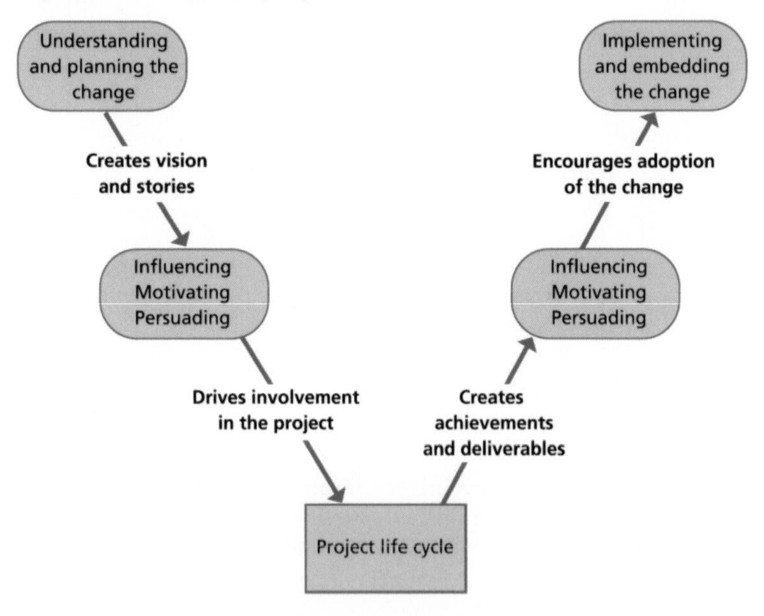

Figure 30: How projects are impacted by change

Integrating change activities into the project life cycle

In order to demonstrate how change management can be improved through stronger links with project management, I have aligned the two disciplines within a simple five-step project life cycle, but my suggestions are applicable to all project life cycles including those defined in PRINCE2® or the bodies of knowledge from the Association for Project Management or the Project Management Institute.

Figure 31: A five-step project life cycle

Rather than define every activity, document, review or decision, I shall examine each stage of the life cycle of a project to find the opportunities for implementing and embedding change.

Concept

The purpose of this stage is to understand the idea that forms the basis of the potential project and define it in sufficient detail for it to be reviewed and evaluated. At the end of this stage, the idea is either rejected, or authorisation is given to define it further.

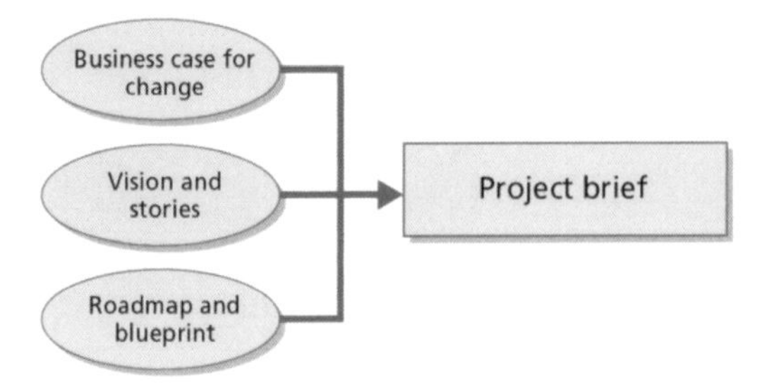

Figure 32: How concept is impacted by aligning the change life cycle

Figure 32 shows how outputs from the change life cycle are essential inputs to the creation of the project brief. The project brief explains the purpose of the project, and this is driven by the requirements of the change, embodied in the vision, stories, roadmap and blueprint.

Concept is an information-gathering stage resulting in a definition of the scope, requirements, objectives, benefits and risks of the project. This information is typically recorded in a project brief or project scope document and is used to decide if the project is viable and worth defining further.

This information is a product of:

- research about the change and the reasons for the business transformation;
- requirements-gathering activities, which provide an opportunity for users to describe what is to be created by the project and how these deliverables will be deployed.

Research about the change

Figure 33 shows how the documents produced to justify the change will not be wholly relevant to the scope and objectives of a specific project, but are a useful source of background information.

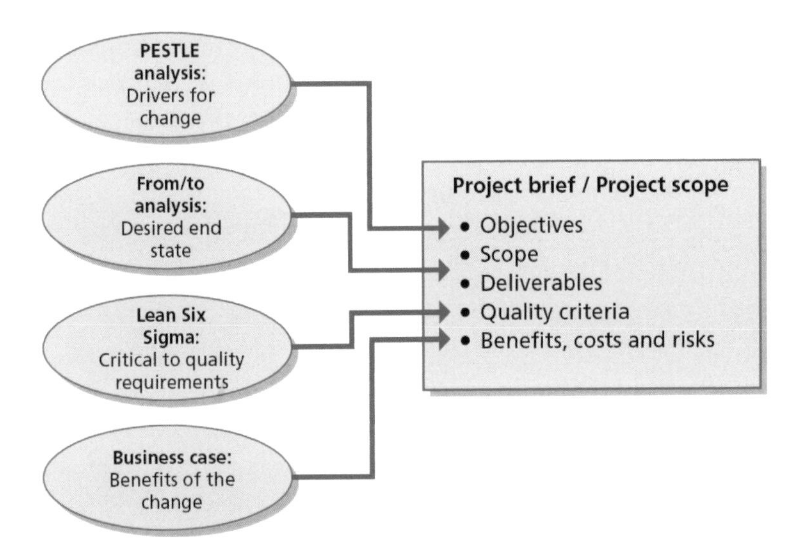

Figure 33: Incorporating change management information into the project description

In my role as project manager, I really enjoy working on projects that have come about through a well-planned change. Objectives and scope are pre-defined as my project has to match what the change is trying to achieve. It is more difficult to work on projects that start out as apparently small-scale 'improvements' but evolve into large-scale change, as more and more needs are identified. Then I feel as if the responsibility for the whole change effort has become my problem, when what we really need is a change manager looking at the implications from an organisation-wide perspective.

Requirements gathering

Requirements gathering involves discussion with all stakeholders to pinpoint what deliverables are needed, which features are most important, what inputs the deliverables require and what outputs they will lead to (e.g. information, decisions or physical items).

To keep the project on schedule, project teams might be tempted to speak to as few stakeholders as possible. However, by asking for this information, the project team are encouraging individuals to begin the transition. The earlier individuals can move through shock, anger and denial into acceptance of the change, the earlier the implementation of the change can begin.

To widen participation in requirements gathering, the project team should enhance interviews and one-to-one meetings with the use of focus groups and workshops. These involve a higher number of participants and have the capacity to generate an energy and engagement with the project and its associated change that is not possible in an interview.

When the idea for the change is first announced, there is likely to be shock and in some cases anger that the current approach is no longer 'fit for purpose'. People are acutely aware of how much they could lose when change happens, and this can make them unwilling to participate in a requirements-gathering exercise. This may be in stark contrast to the project team who are excited to be involved in the project and are looking forward to getting started. The project team needs to give the users an opportunity to vent their anger and to decide for themselves how much to co-operate.

Definition

This stage defines the activities needed to deliver the idea: to prioritise, sequence and resource the activities through the creation of a project plan. The project organisation structure is designed and details of how the project will be managed are defined in a range of strategy documents. This information is contained within a project initiation document or project charter. At the end of this stage, those sponsoring the project can evaluate it and either reject it or authorise its development.

Project plan

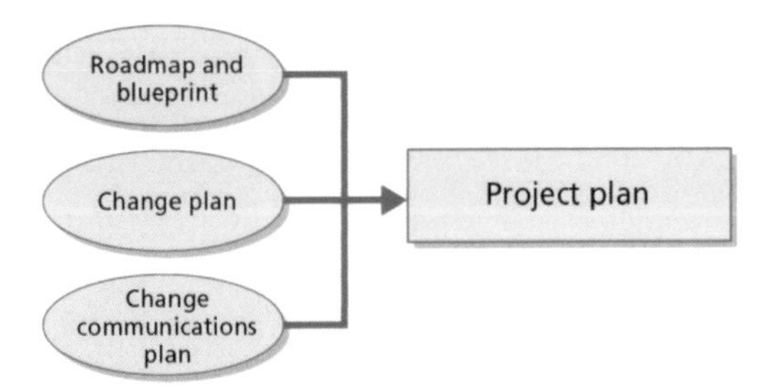

Figure 34: Impact of change management activities on definition

Figure 34 shows how specific change management documents can add vital information to the project plan. For example, the roadmap and blueprint can provide milestones that the project must achieve, and the change plan and change communications plan identify specific activities relating to the implementation of what the project delivers, which will require the involvement of the project team.

There are benefits to be gained from working with the change team in creating a unified project/change plan:

- Those who work in project management have often received extensive training in planning, scheduling and resourcing techniques that can be of benefit to those who are creating the change plans.

- The activities in each plan share common resources so it is sensible to integrate the activities to avoid resource conflicts and minimise disruption to business as usual.
- It removes duplication of effort. This is especially true of communication where there is potential to create confusion amongst the stakeholders if project and change communications are not integrated.

Incorporating change management into the project plan means including more activities, but it also makes available a bigger pool of resources. We can now draw on all those impacted by the implementation of the change. When assigning resources to each activity, ask 'How can I involve people who are part of this change?' Involvement provides individuals with a mechanism to move through the transition curve and increases their ownership, so that they are doing change to themselves rather than having it done to them. There should be no restrictions on the type of activity that can be offered as an opportunity for involvement:

- defining the new business processes;
- defining the information flows and decision points for each new business process;
- defining the functionality of systems and software;
- defining the information fields for screens and reports;
- identifying how quality will be reviewed in the process;
- specifying the quality criteria that processes and systems need to meet.

A lot of the activities identified in the change plan can be incorporated in the project plan, so that whilst the new products and services are being developed, they are also being marketed to the users. These pre-transition activities can support the change on two levels by:

- helping individuals prepare emotionally for the change, using their interaction with the project to move through the transition curve;
- identifying activities to prepare the working environment to be ready for the change. The project is delivering new products and services but they will only realise business benefits if the support mechanism around them is ready. This includes:
  - redefining business processes to take account of new functionality;
  - reorganising roles and responsibilities;
  - preparing the physical and IT infrastructure to be ready to incorporate the new products and services.

Part of project planning involves identifying and analysing the risks. Traditionally this covers risks to the delivery of the project but we need to widen this to include risks of adoption of the change, risk of productivity dip during the implementation of the change and the risk that the change will destabilise the business-as-usual environment. By identifying these risks and identifying the actions needed to mitigate them there is a knock-on effect to the scope of the project plan, as many of these mitigating actions will reside within the business-as-usual environment.

The business case for the project is developed to prove the viability of the project. The benefits are measurable improvements that result from successful delivery of the project, but, in some cases, the creation of the deliverables is only beneficial when it is implemented as part of the overall change. Therefore, the benefits of the project and the benefits of the change may be closely aligned.

The costs of those projects that incorporate change management activities may be higher than those projects that focus solely on delivery. This is because the time taken to involve those impacted by the change is greater and often requires more resources, for example:

- workshops to involve a high number of individuals in requirements gathering, planning, risk analysis and communication activities;
- training significant numbers of people in understanding the deliverables and providing one-to-one user support.

Figure 35 shows that incorporating change activities into the project life cycle can shorten the overall duration of the business transformation as individuals move towards acceptance of the change through their involvement in the project, rather than their transition being triggered at the end of the project.

Overall, the additional costs of incorporating change activities into the project should be outweighed by the shorter time taken to fully embed the change and realise the benefits.

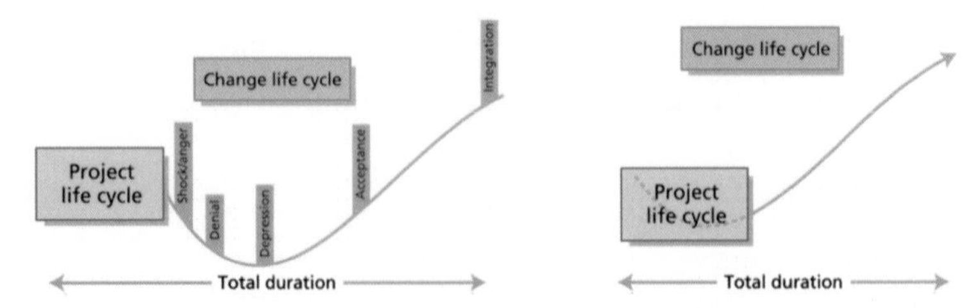

Figure 35: Integration of the project management life cycle and the transition curve

Organisation structure

Organisations that have a successful track record in implementing change align the processes for project and change and the teams responsible for them to a common objective of realising the benefits of the change. This shared responsibility can be reflected in the organisation structure that is created to support transformational change.

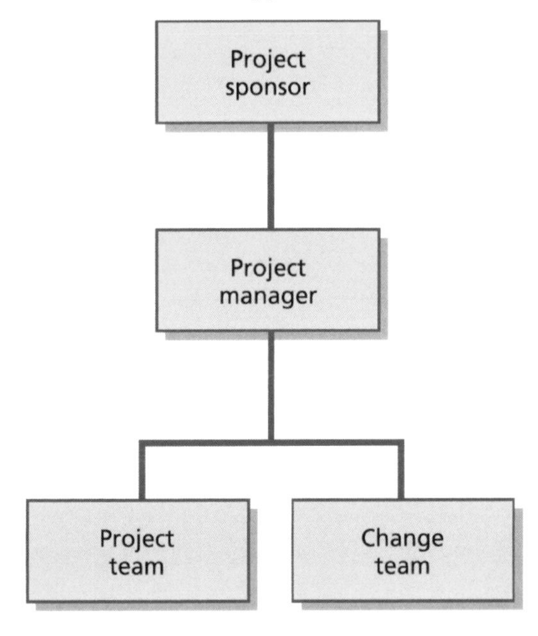

Figures 36: Aligning project and change resources (I)

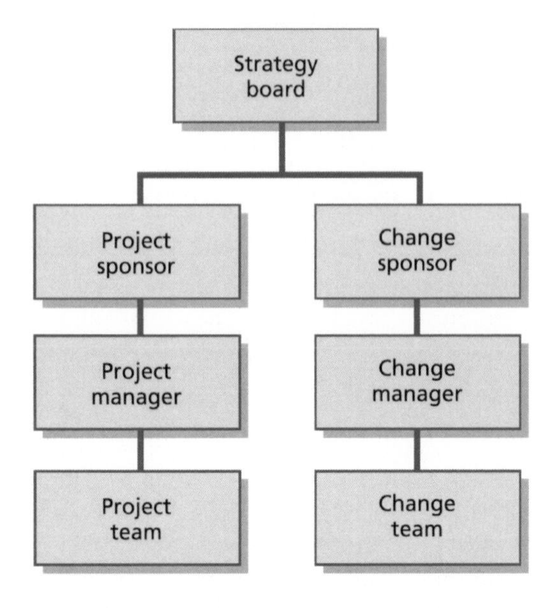

Figures 37: Aligning project and change resources (II)

Figure 36 shows those responsible for the change incorporated into the project organisation structure, whilst in Figure 37, project and change structures share a common senior-level governance structure.

Strategy documents

As part of the project initiation document or project charter, how key elements of the project will be managed are defined, including the approach to risk and issue management, how quality will be managed and how the benefits identified in the project business case will be reviewed and measured.

Benefits from the project cannot be realised unless the project deliverables have been implemented and embedded into the business environment. Therefore, there is a strong link between the activities undertaken within a specific project to deliver benefits and the activities that continue after project closure to ensure that the new ways of working are delivering the improvements expected. Whilst progress on the achievement of benefits will be reviewed throughout the project life cycle, the need to realise benefits from the overall change is the responsibility of the change manager. The change manager and project manager need to work closely together to ensure that their efforts are complementary and not in conflict. If the project is not on course to deliver any benefits, then its viability is questioned; but similarly if the change is poorly communicated and resistance to change is high, then the ability of the project team to deliver benefits is negatively impacted.

Development

The purpose of this stage is to research, design and develop the deliverables. Some of those working in the project team will have been drawn from the user community. Their combined knowledge of the project deliverables and the business environment mean that they can contribute greatly to persuading and influencing their colleagues to become positively engaged with the change.

The project team needs people who can 'walk in the shoes' of those being affected by the change. They can have peer-to-peer conversations with those who are suffering as a result of the change, they can talk the language and explain why the change is going to make life easier, not as a corporate message, but with real proof about real processes.

These project team members can provide the information needed to trigger the development of new roles and responsibilities, new processes and KPIs. Time must be included in the project plan for these individuals to perform their project role and to carry out their relationship role, building a bridge between the work that their former colleagues are doing (the current business as usual) and the results of their project work (the new business as usual).

If the project plan allows time for developing, testing and delivering only, vital opportunities for communication will be lost.

The purpose of these communication activities is to suggest ways in which deliverables from the project can be used to overcome well-known problems within the business-as-usual environment, or to implement ideas that have been talked about and have support, but have never been implemented. It is the up-to-date knowledge of business processes that make these project team members effective communicators, as they have a ready-made rapport with their colleagues and are able to empathise with them and engage with them as a peer group.

Figure 38 shows how activities from the change life cycle continue to be of value throughout the development phase of the project. The stories that individuals use to explain the change can provide a good understanding of how the project deliverables will be used in the business environment. The feedback from stakeholders and the reactions of those adjusting to the change through transition can impact how the deliverables will be used and, therefore, what functions should be examined during quality reviews.

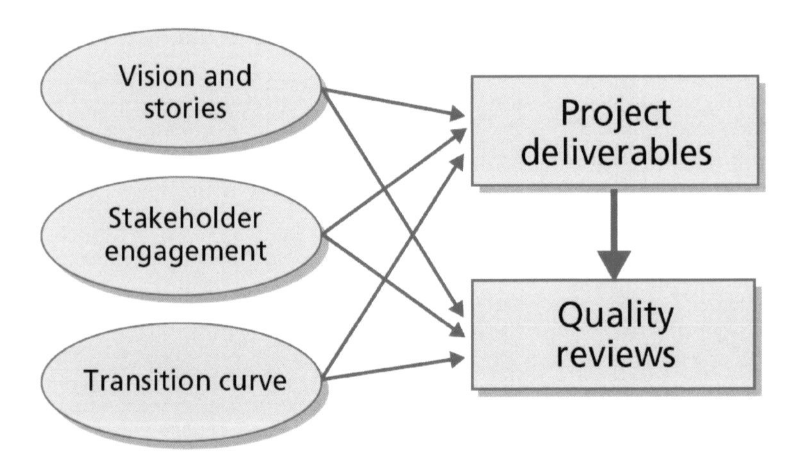

Figure 38: Impact of change management activities on development

During development, the project can become inward looking, concentrating on solving technical problems and ensuring progress is on time and on budget. To retain focus on the alignment of the project and the wider change initiative, the progress reports from project team members and the progress reports from the project manager to the sponsors and senior decision makers should include assessment of the success of the change activities, identifying:

- the level of support for the change;
- the level of adoption that has already taken place;
- the challenges to successful implementation of the project deliverables.

Test

The purpose of this stage is to quality review the deliverables of the project, either as individual components (unit testing), or fitted together as the final integrated product (system testing).

Testing is an opportunity for more users to become involved in the change. Users begin the process of implementing the change by using the testing of how the deliverables operate to define the processes that will surround them. Workshops can be held to define the inputs, processes and outputs that are affected by the new deliverables. This is an opportunity to transfer ownership for the deliverables from the project team, who created them, to those who will be responsible for implementing the change and creating the new business-as-usual environment.

Testing is not only about the quality of what has been produced, but also about whether it is fit for purpose to achieve the desired business gain. What this means in practice is that the product can deliver benefits in the way it can be used, rather than necessarily meeting exactly the original specification that was set for it. This tells us that for the project to contribute effectively to change, there has to be tolerance in the scope and requirements of what is produced.

Test scripts have to be developed that describe how the product is to be used and what the expected outputs are; the questions they ask should be answered with a definitive 'Yes' or 'No'. This encourages testing to investigate the impact of the deliverable on the overall business process rather than testing the presence of specific features –

identifying if use of the product has delivered business benefits.

Another problem is the pressure to accept test results that prove that the product has met the requirements, even if the test indicates that the desired business benefits have not been achieved. The reason for this is that having to go back and rework part of the product in response to a failed test can have a serious impact on the schedule and budget of the project.

Training in the new deliverables usually takes place in this phase of the project life cycle, and this is an excellent opportunity to engage people with the change. The purpose of the training has to widen from 'How does the deliverable work?' to 'How should the deliverable be applied to my work?'

Project training is usually training in the functions, features and uses of the products created by the project. In implementing change, the focus of the training needs to be on how to apply what has been created to business needs. This requires a level of engagement with the anticipated benefits of the change and how processes and working practices will need to alter to make full use of what the project creates. For this reason, training of those involved in implementing the change should take place as early as possible so that they can use their knowledge to feed into the change.

Close

The purpose of this stage is to hand over the deliverables to the users, ensure that all the project documentation has been completed and is ready for archiving, and that all outstanding issues have been closed or have been notified to the users. It is at this point that the project team are released to other work.

During the project, greater understanding of the requirements and the management of risks and issues will have led to amendments to some deliverables, and the need for some deliverables to be removed and new products added. The project team has built up a detailed understanding of the deliverables, including:

- detailed understanding of the inputs and outputs from each of the deliverables;
- the performance of the deliverables under different test conditions;
- minor amendments to the deliverables from their original specification;
- good practice about the way in which the deliverables should be used.

This is often vital information for those managing the change, as it answers many of the typical questions raised by those implementing the change; for example, 'Why does it do this? It would be more useful if it did X; why did the project team not include this feature?' The project team has the answer to the questions, 'How did we get to this point?' and 'Why does the product work this way?'

This knowledge can help those implementing the deliverables to make the detailed changes to their working practices that will realise benefits and create the positive outcomes intended by the change. However, it is often at such a low level of detail that:

- It appears so minor that it is not always captured in the project documentation.

- Those implementing change do not have the time or inclination to trawl through detailed project specifications and test results to find it.

For this reason, closure should include a period of support between some members of the project team and those responsible for implementing change. Contributors to this book outlined their own approach to this:

On any project that we deliver, I schedule for 25% to 30% of the project team to be available for up to a month after go-live. They are available to answer any and every question that users have, but as this doesn't always keep them fully occupied, we schedule preparation work for their next projects during this time.

We call the period between handing over the deliverables and walking away 'the warranty period'. I agree with the department heads how long they want support and then pick a couple of those who worked on the project the longest and know the most to stay around and help the users.

I build this transfer of knowledge into the project plan. A couple of users are selected early in the project to be project liaison officers and they sit with the project team and absorb everything there is to know. They go to every project meeting, they review everything the project team produce and they are responsible for communicating what they know back to their colleagues.

Another critical element of closure is the project review, which establishes if the project has delivered what was required and if it has delivered the benefits that were outlined in the project business case. It is essential the results of this meeting are communicated to those managing the overall change:

- project successes (achievement of benefits, well-received project deliverables) will feed the impetus for making the change;

- shortfalls in expectations will increase the resistance to change.

If possible, the change manager should participate in the reviews and understand the impact of the project at a detailed level, so that any amendments to the change plan can be identified.

CONCLUSION

Numerous studies analysing why some organisations perform better than others have identified change management as a significant contributor to success. Increasingly, we are judged on our ability to adapt to changes initiated by others and to create innovations of our own. We are expected to intuitively understand how change happens because we are a part of change all of the time. However, participating in change may only involve a willingness to be swept along by the knowledge and enthusiasm of others. Leading change requires an ability to analyse and plan the change along with a willingness to address the psychological impact that the change has on ourselves and others.

The techniques and ideas in this book are designed to support you in developing this essential skill set, but they are only the start of your journey. Your effectiveness in managing change requires you to get involved, and to consciously evaluate the impact of your involvement, so that you can refine your approach. I have included lots of techniques in this book because our approach to managing change cannot be bought off the shelf. It has to be adapted, so that it is relevant to the organisation that we are seeking to change. Every activity must be shaped to fit the culture and values of those involved in the change. Every transformational change will be a new experience, and that is what makes this area of business so exciting.

I wish you luck with all of your change activities, and I hope that you are inspired by all that you achieve.

BIBLIOGRAPHY

Alpha Project Managers: What the Top 2% Know That Everyone Else Does Not, Andy Crowe, Velociteach Press (2006), ISBN 0-972-96733-8

Reorganize for Resilience: Putting Customers at the Center of Your Business, Ranjay Gulati, Harvard Business School Press (2010), ISBN 978-1-42211-721-7

Exploring Strategic Change (Exploring Corporate Strategy), Prof. Julia Balogun *et al.*, Pearson Education (2006), ISBN 978-0-273-70802-5

The Definitive Business Plan: The Fast Track to Intelligent Business Planning for Executives and Entrepreneurs, Richard Stutely, Financial Times Series (2002), ISBN 0-273-65921-9

Project Managing Change: Practical Tools and Techniques to Make Change Happen, Ira Blake and Cindy Bush, Financial Times Series (2009), ISBN 978-0-273-72045-4

Informal Learning: Rediscovering the Natural Pathways That Inspire Innovation and Performance, Jay Cross, John Wiley & Sons (2007), ISBN 978-0-7879-8169-3

Our Iceberg is Melting: Change and Succeed Under Adverse Conditions, John Kotter and Holger Rathgeber, Macmillan (2006), ISBN 978-0-23001-420-6

Lean Six Sigma for Dummies, John Morgan, John Wiley & Sons (2009), ISBN 978-0-47075-626-3

The Lean Six Sigma Pocket Toolbook: A Quick Reference Guide to 70 Tools for Improving Quality and Speed, Michael L. George *et al.*, McGraw Hill Professional (2005), ISBN 978-0-07144-119-3

Bibliography

Project Portfolio Management: A Practical Guide to Selecting Projects, Managing Portfolios, and Maximizing Benefits, Max Wideman and Harvey A. Levine, Jossey-Bass Business & Management (2005), ISBN 978-0-78797-754-2

A Guide to the Project Management Body of Knowledge: PMBOK Guide, 4th edn, Project Management Institute (2009), ISBN 978-1-93389-051-7

Making Sense of Change Management: A Complete Guide to the Models Tools and Techniques of Organizational Change, 2nd edn, Cameron and Green, Kogan Page (2009), ISBN 978-0-74945-310-7

Executive Coaching With Backbone and Heart, 2nd edn, Mary Beth O'Neill, Jossey Bass (2007), ISBN 978-0-78798-639-1

Diffusion of Innovation, 5th edn, Everett M. Rogers, Simon & Schuster International (2003), ISBN 978-0-74322-209-9

Experiential Learning, David Kolb, Financial Times/Prentice Hall (1983), ISBN 978-0-13295-261-3

On Death and Dying, Kübler Ross, Simon & Schuster (1997), ISBN 978-0-68483-938-7

Transitions: Understanding and Managing Personal Change, Adam, Hayes and Hopson, Wiley-Blackwell (1977), ISBN 0-855-20129-0

What Leaders Do, Kotter, Harvard Business Review (1999), ISBN 978-0-87584-897-6

The Leadership Mystique, Kets de Vries, Financial Times/ Prentice-Hall (2001), ISBN 978-1-40584-019-4

Managing Change, 5th edn, Burnes, Financial Times/Prentice Hall (2009), ISBN 0-273-71174-1

Leading Change, John P. Kotter, Harvard Business School Press (1996), ISBN 0-875-84747-1

Bibliography

Creating Contagious Commitment, Andrea Shapiro, Strategy Perspective (2003), ISBN 0-974-1028-0-6

Persuasion the Art of Influencing People, 2nd edn, James Borg, Pearson Prentice Hall (2007), ISBN 978-0-279-71299-2

A Sense of Urgency, John Kotter, Harvard Business Press (2008), ISBN 978-1-4221-7971-0

Working With Emotional Intelligence, Daniel Goleman, Bloomsbury (1996), ISBN 978-0-7475-2830-2

Influence, the Pyschology of Persuasion, Robert Cialdini, HarperBusiness, Collins Business Essentials (2007), ISBN 978-0-06124-189-5

Resolving Social Conflicts / Field Theory in Social Science, Kurt Lewin, American Psychological Association (1997), ISBN 978-1-55798-415-9

Organizational Transitions: Understanding Complex Change, Richard Beckhardt and Reuben T. Harris, Addison-Wesley (1987), ISBN 978-20110-887-3

The Irrational Side of Change Management, Carolyn Aiken and Scott Keller, McKinsey Quarterly, 2 (2009)

Mind Maps for Business: Revolutionise Your Business Thinking and Practise, Tony Buzan and Chris Griffiths, BBC Active (2009), ISBN 978-1-40664-290-2

Managing Successful Programmes, TSO (2007), ISBN 978-0-11-331040-1

APM Body of Knowledge, 5th edn, Association of Project Management (2006), ISBN 978-1-903494-13-4

ITG RESOURCES

IT Governance Ltd. sources, creates and delivers products and services to meet the real-world, evolving IT governance needs of today's organisations, directors, managers and practitioners. The ITG website (*www.itgovernance.co.uk*) is the international one-stop shop for corporate and IT governance information, advice, guidance, books, tools, training and consultancy.

www.itgovernance.co.uk/catalog/715 is the category page on our website that gives details all of our soft skills titles.

Other websites

Books and tools published by IT Governance Publishing (ITGP) are available from all business booksellers and are also immediately available from the following websites:

www.itgovernance.co.uk/catalog/355 provides information and online purchasing facilities for every currently available book published by ITGP.

http://www.itgovernance.eu is our euro-denominated website which ships from Benelux and has a growing range of books in European languages other than English.

www.itgovernanceusa.com is a US$-based website that delivers the full range of IT Governance products to North America, and ships from within the continental US.

www.itgovernanceasia.com provides a selected range of ITGP products specifically for customers in South Asia.

www.27001.com is the IT Governance Ltd. website that deals specifically with information security management, and ships from within the continental US.

Pocket guides

For full details of the entire range of pocket guides, simply follow the links at *www.itgovernance.co.uk/publishing.aspx*.

Toolkits

ITG's unique range of toolkits includes the IT Governance Framework Toolkit, which contains all the tools and guidance that you will need in order to develop and implement an appropriate IT governance framework for your organisation. Full details can be found at *www.itgovernance.co.uk/products/519*.

For a free paper on how to use the proprietary Calder-Moir IT Governance Framework, and for a free trial version of the toolkit, see *www.itgovernance.co.uk/calder_moir.aspx*.

There is also a wide range of toolkits to simplify implementation of management systems, such as an ISO/IEC 27001 ISMS or a BS25999 BCMS, and these can all be viewed and purchased online at:
http://www.itgovernance.co.uk/catalog/1.

Best Practice Reports

ITG's range of Best Practice Reports is now at *www.itgovernance.co.uk/best-practice-reports.aspx*. These offer you essential, pertinent, expertly researched information on a number of key issues including Web 2.0 and Green IT.

Training and consultancy

IT Governance also offers training and consultancy services across the entire spectrum of disciplines in the information governance arena. Details of training courses can be accessed at *www.itgovernance.co.uk/training.aspx* and descriptions of our consultancy services can be found at *http://www.itgovernance.co.uk/consulting.aspx*. Why not contact us to see how we could help you and your organisation?

Newsletter

IT governance is one of the hottest topics in business today, not least because it is also the fastest moving, so what better way to keep up than by subscribing to ITG's free monthly newsletter *Sentinel*? It provides monthly updates and resources across the whole spectrum of IT governance subject matter, including risk management, information security, ITIL and IT service management, project governance, compliance and so much more. Subscribe for your free copy at: *www.itgovernance.co.uk/newsletter.aspx*.